PUTTING OUR HOUSE IN ORDER

RECASTING G8 POLICY TOWARDS AFRICA

DAVID MEPHAM AND JAMES LORGE

The ippr

The Institute for Public Policy Research (ippr) is the UK's leading progressive think tank and was established in 1988. Its role is to bridge the political divide between the social democratic and liberal traditions, the intellectual divide between academia and the policy making establishment and the cultural divide between government and civil society. It is first and foremost a research institute, aiming to provide innovative and credible policy solutions. Its work, the questions its research poses and the methods it uses are driven by the belief that the journey to a good society is one that places social justice, democratic participation and economic and environmental sustainability at its core.

For further information you can contact ippr's external affairs department on info@ippr.org, you can view our website at www.ippr.org and you can buy our books from Central Books on 0845 458 9910 or email ippr@centralbooks.com.

Our trustees

CONTENTS

Acknowledgements

The ippr would like to thank Anglo American plc, the International HIV/ AIDS Alliance, Pfizer Inc., Save the Children, Shell International and the UK Prime Minister's Strategy Unit for their generous financial support for this ippr research project. The report represents the views of the authors, not those of our funders.

Special thanks to Simon Retallack (ippr) for his considerable contribution to the climate change chapter. Thanks also to Leni Wild (ippr), Tony Grayling (ippr) and Tim Gibbs (ippr) for their contribution to the climate change chapter. Many thanks to Bronwen Manby (Open Society Institute), Nick Pearce (ippr) and Howard Reed (ippr) for their extensive comments on the report.

Thanks to Edward Bickham (Anglo American plc), Ken Bluestone (VSO), Ben Carrick (Pfizer Inc.), Laurence Cockcroft (Transparency International), Alan Detheridge (Shell International), Patricia Feeney (RAID), Penny Fowler (Oxfam), Romilly Greenhill (ActionAid), Caroline Halmshaw (International HIV/AIDS Alliance), Susan Hawley (Corner House), John Hilary (War on Want), Glenys Kinnock MEP, Jan Kiso (UK Prime Minister's Strategy Unit), Joseph Miller (Saferworld), Paul Clough (ippr), Diarmid O'Sullivan (Global Witness), Ruchi Tripathi (ActionAid) and Hennie van Vuuren (Institute for Security Studies) for their comments.

Thanks to John Schwartz (ippr) and Nicholas Thorner (ippr) for their help with the publication of this report.

Some of the ideas in this report were generated from a series of useful meetings in South Africa. Thanks to the UK High Commission in South Africa, the Institute for Security Studies, the South African Institute for International Affairs, IDASA, SaferAfrica and the Human Sciences Research Council for giving us their time and sharing their thoughts.

About the authors

David Mepham is an Associate Director and Head of the International Programme at ippr. From 1998 to 2002, he was a special adviser within the UK's Department for International Development. Prior to this, David ran the British Foreign Policy programme for the independent foreign affairs think tank Saferworld from 1997 to 1998. From 1994 to 1997, David was the international policy specialist in the Labour Party's policy department.

David is the author of four ippr reports and co-editor of 'A New Deal for Africa' (*New Economy*, 2004). He is a frequent commentator on international issues in the press and broadcast media.

James Lorge is a Research Fellow for the International Programme at the ippr. Prior to this he was the Africa Desk Officer at the Forum on Early Warning and Early Response (FEWER) working on conflict prevention issues. He has also worked in Angola, the Democratic Republic of Congo and Rwanda with Médecins sans Frontières and Merlin.

James also co-edited 'A New Deal for Africa' (*New Economy*, 2004).

About ippr's International Programme

ippr's International Programme was created in July 2002. Its aim is to apply the ippr's core values of social justice, opportunity and sustainability to some of the most pressing global issues and to formulate practical policy responses to them. The programme seeks to make a policy contribution in four broad areas: global security, poverty reduction and sustainable development, human rights, and national and global governance.

For further information about the programme's work please visit www. ippr.org/international. The programme is supported by an International Advisory Group, including: Professor Kevin Boyle (Essex University Human Rights Centre), Hubert Danso (africapractice), Richard Dowden (Royal Africa Society), Stefanie Grant (Harrison Grant Solicitors), David Held (LSE), Richard Jolly (Honorary Professorial Fellow and Research Associate, Institute for Development Studies), Glenys Kinnock MEP, Bronwen Manby (Open Society Foundation), Andrew Puddephatt (Director of Global Partners and Associates), Lord Bhikhu Parekh.

Acronyms

ACP	African, Caribbean and Pacific countries
AFLEG	Africa Law Enforcement and Governance
AGOA	Africa Growth and Opportunity Act
APRM	African Peer Review Mechanism
ARV	Anti-retroviral treatment
AU	African Union
CAP	Common Agricultural Policy
DAC	Development Assistance Committee
DFID	UK Department for International Development
DRC	Democratic Republic of Congo
EBA	Everything But Arms
ECAs	Export Credit Agencies
EITI	Extractive Industries Transparency Initiative
EPA	Economic Partnership Agreement
ESAAMLG	Eastern and Southern Africa Anti-Money Laundering Group
EU	European Union
EUC	End User Certificate
FATF	Financial Action Task Force
FLEGT	Forest Law Enforcement, Governance and Trade
GBS	General Budget Support
GDP	Gross Domestic Product
GSPs	Generalised System of Preferences
HIPC	Heavily Indebted Poor Countries initiative
IFF	International Finance Facility
IFIs	International Financial Institutions
IMF	International Monetary Fund
IPCC	Intergovernmental Panel on Climate Change
LDCs	Least Developed Countries
LICUS	Low Income Countries Under Stress
MAP	World Bank's Multi-country HIV/AIDS Program
MATCH	The ad hoc group for the modelling and assessment of contributions to climate change
MDGs	Millennium Development Goals
NCP	National Contact Point
NEPAD	New Partnership for Africa's Development
NGO	Non-governmental Organisation
OAU	Organisation of African Unity
OECD	Organisation for Economic Co-operation and Development
PEPFAR	US President's Emergency Plan for AIDS Relief
PRBS	Poverty Reduction Budget Support
PRS	Poverty Reduction Strategy

PRSP	Poverty Reduction Strategy Paper
PSIA	Poverty and Social Impact Analysis
PV	Photovoltaic
REEEP	Renewable Energy and Energy Efficiency Partnership
SBS	Sector Budget Support
SFO	Serious Fraud Office
TRIPS	Agreement on Trade Related Aspects of Intellectual Property
UNAIDS	The Joint UN Programme on HIV/AIDS
UNCTAD	United Nations Conference on Trade and Development
UNECA	United Nations Economic Commission for Africa
UNFCCC	United Nations Framework Convention on Climate Change
WHO	World Health Organisation
WTO	World Trade Organisation

Executive summary

While Africa is a large and extremely diverse continent, and while some of its countries are making significant development progress, too many of its people are being left behind. Just under half of Africa's population is living on less than a dollar a day (the World Bank's headcount measure of extreme poverty), 300 million Africans are malnourished, forty-four million of the continent's children do not go to school, and twenty-eight million Africans are infected with HIV/AIDS. The HIV/AIDS pandemic constitutes not just an African health crisis, but a humanitarian, social, political and security one – cutting life expectancies in some countries by fifty per cent, reversing development gains built up over decades and weakening government systems. During the last two decades, Africa has also been the continent most affected by violent conflict.

On current trends, there is no prospect of Africa achieving the Millennium Development Goals (MDGs) – the set of targets for poverty reduction and development agreed by the governments of the world at the UN Millennium Summit in 2000. These goals are supposed to be obtained by 2015. But at existing rates of progress they are unlikely to be met in Africa for over a hundred years, and they will not be met at all if the HIV/ AIDS pandemic is not tackled effectively.

An important part of the explanation and responsibility for the condition of Africa rests with Africa's elites and with the state of politics and governance across the continent. This has too often been denied or downplayed by progressives in developed countries, who have tended to depoliticise the development process or to put exclusive emphasis on external economic relationships. Over recent decades there have been many cases in which these elites have pursued ruinous economic and social policies that have impoverished their people, widened inequality and increased injustice and discrimination. In some cases, Africa's elites have been blatantly predatory, amassing enormous wealth for themselves and their associates through theft and corruption.

These profound failings of governance and politics in many African states since independence – and the need to develop more capable states – are now openly acknowledged by reformers amongst African governments, civil society, the private sector and regional organisations. The formation of the New Partnership for Africa's Development (NEPAD) in 2001 signalled a clear intention on the part of a group of African countries to break with the mistakes of the past. The launch of the African Union (AU) in 2002 has been another positive development, with the AU making clear commitments to promote better governance across the continent. There is also some evidence of improvements in governance in many African countries in recent years.

But if Africa's governments and people must take more responsibility for the state of their continent, so too must the governments of rich countries, including the G8. Too often, Africa's development plight is seen as an exclusively internal phenomenon in need of an external remedy. Yet some of the policies currently pursued by G8 countries are actually damaging Africa. Other G8 policies are hindering rather than helping Africa to achieve better governance and greater progress in development.

These 'harmful' G8 policies are the specific subject of this report. It is worth briefly explaining this focus. There are, of course, many good things that G8 and other developed countries can do with and for Africa, for example strengthening Africa's capacity to manage conflict, providing resources to tackle HIV/AIDS and other diseases, and supporting institutions such as the African Union. This is a major focus of the work of the Commission for Africa, set up by the UK Government in 2004 and due to report in early 2005. However, the extent to which the existing policies of G8 countries may be damaging Africa is an area that still receives too little attention. But it is the area where G8 countries have least excuse for inaction and where the benefits of better policy could be most far-reaching. As an absolute priority, G8 countries should 'put their own house in order' and end those policies that stymie Africa's development. There are five areas in particular where this is necessary.

Firstly, aid and conditionality. While Africa needs significantly more aid, not least to tackle the HIV/AIDS pandemic and to help meet the MDGs, donor aid has sometimes served to strengthen local elites and done too little to improve the lives of ordinary Africans. In other circumstances, aid has left African governments more accountable to external actors than to their own people. Aid has also been used to promote the commercial objectives of G8 donors through tied aid, or to leverage policy reforms through inappropriate conditionality that have had adverse effects on Africa's poor. And the way in which aid is delivered often imposes very significant transaction costs on African societies.

Secondly, international trade rules. These rules are heavily stacked against Africa's interests. EU and US agricultural subsidies and the dumping of surplus agricultural produce is destroying the livelihoods of large numbers of African farmers. African exporters still have restricted access to developed country markets. Many African countries also suffer the effects of tariff escalation, with countries such as Ghana facing much higher tariffs on processed chocolate than on unprocessed cocoa beans when they try and export into developed country markets. Another trade agreement, the Agreement on Trade Related Aspects of Intellectual Property (TRIPS), has the effect of pushing up the cost of technology and other essential goods, including the price of drugs for treating HIV/AIDS.

Thirdly, arms proliferation. G8 countries are significant suppliers of weapons and military equipment to Africa. Some of these arms are fuelling and exacerbating armed conflicts or strengthening repressive regimes or rebel groups in Africa. Weapons and ammunition are also transferred to Africa by arms brokers, traffickers and transport agents from G8 countries, and G8 governments have still not put in place adequate controls to curb this trade.

Fourthly, corruption and conflict financing. G8 companies have an important role to play in helping Africa to make greater progress in the reduction of poverty and the achievement of the MDGs. But poor governance of the international corporate sector can also damage and distort Africa's development prospects. Despite widespread bribery in Africa involving western companies, G8 governments have done far too little to implement their commitments under the OECD Convention on Combating Bribery of Foreign Public Officials. Nor has enough been done to tackle the role of G8 governments and companies in financing conflict in Africa through the purchase of commodities such as oil, diamonds or timber.

Fifthly, climate change. G8 countries account for around fifty per cent of greenhouse gas emissions, with the US the worst offender, and yet climate variability in the future will disproportionately impact upon Africa. This will be enormously damaging to the continent's prospects for development.

On all these issues – aid and conditionality, trade, arms transfers, corruption and conflict financing, and climate change – G8 countries need to take action. Greater political will on the part of G8 governments is critical to secure the necessary changes in policy. But this is more likely to occur if there is sustained public pressure on them to act differently, and if they are held properly to account for their policies towards Africa. Increasingly, African countries are being urged to be more accountable and to subject their policies to external evaluation, for example through the NEPAD Peer Review Mechanism. But there is no truly comparable process for G8 countries.

In recent years, there have been a number of proposals to address what is often described as 'policy incoherence' towards Africa, on the part of wealthier countries such as the G8. The key concern has been that developed countries should not take away with one hand what they give with the other, and that they should ensure that their broader economic and foreign policies – in areas such as trade, investment or arms exports – are consistent with their stated objectives for international development.

Of course, policy coherence for development is not easy to implement. All governments are trying to fulfil multiple objectives at any one time, and these objectives will often conflict. However, better processes of decision-making can make these choices and tensions more transparent. What is important is that these choices and costs of G8 policy incoherence towards Africa should be openly acknowledged, debated and addressed.

This is not happening at present. Genuinely independent reporting, better analysis and a refined methodology for assessing coherence issues – these could all help in holding G8 countries to account. However, the real obstacles to better policy towards Africa on the part of the G8 are not technical but political. Africa's interests, and the harmful impacts of G8 policy on Africa, need to be pushed higher up the international political agenda, and mechanisms developed for sustaining that concern over time.

One way to help achieve this would be through the establishment of a new G8/Africa Forum. This would replace the current unstructured dialogue between G8 and African leaders and become a formal and permanent part of the annual G8 Summit. This Forum should bring together political leaders from the G8 and Africa, as well as the UN Secretary General and the heads of international and regional financial institutions. To ensure that these issues are taken seriously at the very highest levels within Africa and the G8, a report should be presented by the UN Secretary General. This should be a detailed checklist that looks at the implementation of existing commitments, particularly at 'coherence' issues. G8 countries should be required to respond in detail to the report.

G8 countries have a clear moral responsibility to end those policies that leave Africa disadvantaged. But it is also in their interests to do so. The consequences of Africa's poverty will not remain confined within Africa's borders. Poverty and underdevelopment create fertile conditions for a new set of security threats, including violent conflict, crime and terrorism, the spread of disease, and the trafficking of people, arms and illicit drugs. A more stable, prosperous and democratic Africa would also bring enormous benefits, opening up opportunities for mutually beneficial trade, investment and cultural exchange and the more effective management of common problems. Moreover, many of the obstacles to better G8 policy towards Africa are economic and financial vested interests in G8 countries. Taking on these vested interests will often be beneficial to G8 consumers as well as to Africa.

2005 represents a real opportunity to make substantive progress on these 'coherence' issues that matter so much to Africa. The UK Government has the presidencies of the EU and the G8 in this year, and has already indicated that Africa will be a priority for international action. The Commission for Africa, set up by the UK Government, will report in early 2005. The September UN Review Conference on progress towards the MDGs will also ensure that development issues and the needs of Africa will remain a central focus of international political attention. And 2005 marks the 20th anniversary of Live Aid, encouraging a much wider group of people to engage – perhaps some for the first time – with issues around Africa and global justice, including through the non-governmental organisation (NGO) campaign 'Make Poverty History'.

G8 countries need to rise to this challenge: to end those policies that stymie Africa's development prospects and to build a deeper and more equitable partnership with the continent for development, capable states and peace.

Key policy recommendations

1. Rethinking aid and conditionality

G8 countries should:

- Commit to reaching the UN 0.7 per cent aid/national income target by 2010 and set up the International Finance Facility (IFF) as soon as possible.

- Substantially increase funding for tackling HIV/AIDS to help improve access to prevention, care and treatment services, including a huge increase in the provision of anti-retrovirals; support the strengthening of African healthcare systems and civil society groups working to combat the disease; and provide donor support in line with the 'Three Ones' principles.

- Untie all bilateral aid to all African countries, simplify reporting requirements and implement the Rome Declaration on good donor practice, including more predictable levels of aid funding.

- Support 100 per cent multilateral debt cancellation for low-income African countries that demonstrate that they will use the proceeds to reduce poverty.

- Promote a new approach to conditionality linked to African governments' own development goals and their Poverty Reduction Strategies (PRSs), and promote a less rigid approach to macro-economic stability within the International Financial Institutions.

2. Supporting fairer global rules of trade

G8 countries should:

- Phase out all agricultural export subsidies.

- End tariff escalation (the practice of putting higher tariffs on processed and semi-processed goods), to help African countries to reduce their dependence on primary commodities.

- Introduce simple and liberal 'rules of origin', so that African countries can source their inputs from the most competitive suppliers and derive greater benefits from trade preferences.

- Reform existing intellectual property rules to enable African and other poor countries to import generic versions of patented drugs; where possible, to issue compulsory licences for the production of drugs; and not introduce, under any circumstances, TRIPS-plus measures into bilateral free trade agreements with African countries.

- Allow African, Caribbean and Pacific (ACP) countries to determine the degree and pace of market opening, consistent with their broader development strategies, in the current negotiations with the EU on the proposed Economic Partnership Agreements (EPAs).

3. Restricting arms transfers

G8 countries should:

- Establish an International Arms Trade Treaty, setting high common standards governing arms transfers to conflict-affected regions in Africa and elsewhere.

- Agree common extra-territorial controls over arms brokers and push for a binding international agreement on arms brokering at the 2006 UN Review Conference on Small Arms, and introduce a compulsory registration scheme for arms brokers and transport agents.

4. Curbing corruption and conflict financing

G8 countries should:

- Close loopholes in the OECD Convention on Combating Bribery of Foreign Public Officials, ratify the UN Convention against Corruption and provide additional resources to investigate and prosecute G8 companies that engage in corruption abroad.

- Deny export credit guarantees, government procurement and other forms of government support, for a specified period, to companies found to have engaged in corrupt practices abroad.

- Press the International Financial Institutions to develop a model template for the governance of natural resource revenues and to promote revenue transparency by governments and companies in all the resource-rich African countries they work with.

5. Addressing climate change

G8 countries should:

- Commit to global emission reductions of fifteen per cent below 2000 levels or ten per cent below 1990 levels by 2020, and build support for international action that will keep temperature increases to no more than 2°C above pre-industrial levels.

- Provide increased funding for African countries to adapt to current levels of climate change, and ensure that adaptation issues are mainstreamed into all forms of development assistance.

Conclusion – holding G8 countries to account

G8 countries should:

- Establish a new G8/Africa Forum – bringing together political leaders from the G8 and Africa, as well as the UN Secretary General, and the heads of the International Financial Institutions (IFIs) and the African Development Bank – and make this a permanent part of the G8 Summit.

- Make the UNECA/OECD-DAC biennial report a central focus of discussions at the G8 Africa Forum; a checklist of commitments made to Africa and of progress in implementing them, with a particular focus on coherence issues.

- Subject important areas of their policy – for example on trade, investment and arms exports – to a comprehensive 'development audit'.

Introduction

Although Africa's problems are often described as home-grown, anyone familiar with the history of colonial and post-colonial relations between Africa and the rich world knows that the two are inextricably linked. Policies made in Brussels, London and Washington often have direct impacts on African farmers, on the employment prospects of young African men and women and on African governments' capacity to pay their bills.

K.Y. Amoako, Executive Secretary, United Nations Economic
Commission for Africa (2004)

2005 will be a milestone in our campaign to meet the Millennium Development Goals. And it will be the year that will test the might of our resolve – and the commitment of the whole international community – to progress towards a more just and secure world.

Rt Hon. Gordon Brown, UK Chancellor of the Exchequer
(September 2004)

Nowhere are the problems of poverty, weak governance, disease and violent conflict more acute than in Africa. While Africa is a large and extremely diverse continent, and while some of its countries are making significant development progress, too many of its people are being left behind. Just under half of the continent's people are living on less than a dollar a day (the World Bank's headcount measure of extreme poverty), and many African states have lower per capita income today than two decades ago (Herbst and Mills, 2003). A further 300 million Africans are malnourished, forty-four million of the continent's children do not go to school, and twenty-eight million Africans are infected with HIV/AIDS (UNDP, 2003).

The HIV/AIDS pandemic constitutes not just an African health crisis, but a humanitarian, social, political and security one – cutting life expectancies in some countries by fifty per cent, reversing development gains built up over decades and weakening government systems. During the last two decades, Africa has also been the most conflict affected region in the world. In 2003, the UN estimated that twenty-three countries in sub-Saharan Africa 'were experiencing some kind of conflict emergency' resulting in 'several hundred thousands of deaths, especially of children and women, vast population movements, malnutrition, and the wider propagation of diseases such as HIV/AIDS, tuberculosis, malaria, acute respiratory infections and intestinal disorders, not to mention sheer human suffering' (Herbst and Mills, 2003). Moreover, '120,000 child soldiers, out of a global total of 300,000, are said to be participating in various African wars' (*ibid*).

Not surprisingly, there is no prospect on current trends of Africa achieving the MDGs – the set of targets for poverty reduction and development agreed by the governments of the world at the UN Millennium Summit in 2000. These goals include halving the number of people living in poverty, achieving universal primary education, reducing infant and maternal mortality by two-thirds and three-quarters respectively, and halting the spread of HIV/AIDS. All of these goals are supposed to be obtained by 2015. But at existing rates of progress they are unlikely to be met in Africa for over 100 years (Brown, 2004). And they will not be met at all if the HIV/AIDS pandemic is not tackled effectively

An important part of the explanation and responsibility for the condition of Africa rests with Africa's elites and with the state of politics and governance across the continent. This has too often been denied or downplayed by progressives in developed countries, who have tended to depoliticise the development process or to put exclusive emphasis on external economic relationships. Over recent decades there have been many cases in which Africa's elites have pursued ruinous economic and social policies that have impoverished their people, widened inequality and increased injustice and discrimination. In some cases, these elites have been blatantly predatory, amassing enormous wealth for themselves and their associates through theft and corruption (van de Walle, 2001; Rotberg, 2002; Chabal and Daloz, 1999; Bayart *et al.*, 1999). And many of the worst cases of human rights violations on the continent have been carried out by some of Africa's elites against a section of their own people (Cilliers, 2004; HRW, 2004). Understanding African states and African politics – and the relationship between these states and the wider international community – is therefore crucial to understanding the condition of much of Africa today.

The state of the African state

While acknowledging the heterogeneity of state formation across the continent, there are some important common characteristics shared by many African states. The colonial experience meant that a large number of African states were established juridically but not empirically (Jackson, 1990). In essence, these new entities were artificial creations that did not emerge from any long process of state formation, as experienced, for example, in western Europe. These states therefore had very weak foundations. The colonial experience in Africa was distinct from other regions as indigenous political institutions were more comprehensively destroyed. Many African states also inherited at independence a colonial political system that operated by military force, did not institutionalise checks on executive power and was primarily extractive by nature. Some have argued, therefore, that the origin of the style of politics that large numbers of Africans have known since independence lies very much in this colonial experience (Ellis, 2004).

Others have seen post-independence African states as combining the authoritarian legacy of the colonial administration and the African village tradition, and have defined such state systems as neo-patrimonial (Chabal and Daloz, 1999; van de Walle, 2001). By this they mean a clientelistic system of governance based on vertical links of patronage between the political elite and their client constituencies. Access to state resources strengthened this relationship, with Africa's elites able to reward supporters on a scale not seen before. African states often experienced a marked centralisation of power, with 'loyalty to the leader not the country', a blurring of the distinction between the public and the private spheres, and the creation of conditions ripe for corruption and the misuse of public resources (Dowden, 2004).

More recently, commentators and policy-makers have talked about the phenomenon of state weakness or failure in Africa. This takes different forms and goes under a variety of different labels: 'failed states', 'failing states', 'poor performers', 'Low Income Countries under Stress' (LICUS), 'Countries at Risk of Instability' and 'fragile states' are just some of the terms that have been used (Rotberg, 2003; Straw, 2002; World Bank; UK Prime Minister's Strategy Unit, 2005; DFID, 2005).

Many African countries exhibit varying degrees of state weakness and failure. This might best be seen as a continuum, with countries differentiated and defined in terms of their capacity or willingness to deliver on basic 'public goods' (Rotberg, 2003). These 'public goods' include the security of people and their property, health and education services, effective infrastructure, the rule of law, the enjoyment of human rights and democratic freedoms, and a free press and media. 'Capable' states are those that deliver these basic public goods to their citizens. 'Failed states' – like the Democratic Republic of the Congo (DRC), Somalia and Liberia – are those in which the capacity to deliver these public goods has all but disappeared. These countries have effectively disintegrated as a consequence of civil conflict or external invasion. In the case of Somalia, there is no central government at all; while in the DRC the writ of the central government barely extends beyond the capital – much of the rest of the territory is controlled by competing armed groups. Most African states sit along the spectrum in between. They may have weak institutions and bad or weak political leadership; suffer from ethnic, communal, linguistic or religious tensions; experience corruption or conflict; and have inadequate and deteriorating infrastructures and poor quality public services (Kpundeh and Levy, 2004).

In defining its own term – 'fragile states' – the UK's Department for International Development (DFID) has suggested that countries might be seen as falling into four broad types: those with capacity and political will to improve the circumstances of their people; countries that are willing to do so but lack capacity; countries that have capacity but little concern to improve their people's lives (often these states are repressive); and, finally, countries where both capacity and political will are absent (DFID, 2005). Of course, not all African states will fall neatly into these categories. But this framework does usefully highlight the specific challenges posed by fragile states and the huge barrier they represent to more effective development progress in Africa.

On almost any definition, levels of poverty are far worse in fragile states than in countries with stronger political institutions (*ibid*). Levels of child and maternal mortality and diseases such as malaria are higher. Levels of illiteracy are higher and school completion lower. Fragile states are poorer at protecting human rights or tackling crime and lawlessness. Economic growth rates in fragile states also tend to be lower (*ibid*).

Developing capable states in Africa

The profound failings of governance and politics in many African states since independence – and the need to develop more capable states – are now openly acknowledged by reformers amongst African governments, civil society, the private sector and regional organisations. The signing of the New Partnership for Africa's Development (NEPAD) in 2001 signalled a clear intention on the part of a group of African countries to break with the mistakes of the past. As the founding NEPAD statement put it: 'Post-colonial Africa inherited weak states and dysfunctional economies that were further aggravated by poor leadership, corruption and bad governance in many countries' (NEPAD, 2001).

The countries subscribing to NEPAD are committed to pursue a new development strategy in Africa based on good governance and respect for human rights, better conditions for private investment and trade, action against corruption, and greater regional economic integration. They have also established the African Peer Review Mechanism (APRM), with the aim of encouraging better governance, economic development and a strength-ening of the capacity of African states. So far twenty-four African countries have signed up to the process. Under the APRM countries are expected to subject themselves to the scrutiny of their peers through a process involving consultations with government, NGOs and the private sector. They will also be required to develop a programme of action with clear timeframes and objectives. Although the APRM is new and untested (like NEPAD itself), it is an important and innovative development with real potential. A critical issue for the initiative will be the extent to which the review process is genu-inely opened up, for example by giving African civil society a better oppor-tunity to hold their governments to account (Juma, 2004; Cilliers, 2004).

The launch of the African Union (AU) in 2002 has been another positive development. It is guided by a strong Vision and Mission document that sets out very clearly many of the problems facing the continent. This was developed through a properly consultative process with a wide range of African thinkers. In two years, the AU has shown itself to be a more assertive and competent organisation than its predecessor, the Organisation of African Unity (OAU). The AU has played an important role in stabilising Liberia and Burundi, and the establishment of the African Peace and Security Council suggests a willingness to tackle violent conflict in Africa more effectively than in the past. The AU has also committed itself to promoting better governance across the continent (African Union, 2004).

There is also some evidence of improvements in governance in many African countries in recent years. This is revealed, for example, in the findings of a major continent-wide study carried out by the United Nations Economic Commission for Africa (UNECA, 2004). This study reviewed the governance performance of twenty-eight countries against specific criteria, with a wide range of different stakeholders involved in the process. Three positive developments were highlighted by the study. Firstly, that in recent years there has been an important shift towards democratic rule on the continent, with elections now increasingly seen as the only legitimate form of choosing and changing governments. Secondly, there has been a move towards greater openness and accountability, with many African governments conceding greater space for civil society to participate in the political process. One manifestation of this is the growth of independent media on the continent (Karikari, 2004). Thirdly, there have been improvements to economic and financial management in many African countries. This involves countries running smaller deficits, managing tax systems better, improving fiscal transparency and creating institutions for better auditing (UNECA, 2004). These are real grounds for optimism. But the review also stressed how much more needs to be done in many countries to strengthen public administration, the legislature and the judiciary, to tackle corruption and to create a better environment for inward investment and domestic economic activity.

While these developments are welcome, African governments still face massive new challenges in achieving more effective development and better governance, none more so than the HIV/AIDS pandemic.

The challenge of HIV/AIDS

It is hard to overstate the scale of the challenge that HIV/AIDS represents for Africa. It massively complicates the task of promoting more capable states and greater progress in development.

There are an estimated twenty-eight million people living with HIV in Africa. On average, seven to eight per cent of the adult population is infected, with prevalence rates reaching as high as forty per cent in some countries. The vast majority of those living with HIV are not even aware of their HIV status. This is due to a combination of factors, including the fear of stigma and discrimination and lack of access to voluntary HIV counselling and testing. For those who are infected, care and treatment services are extremely limited (Bermejo, 2004). In 2003, the World Health Organisation (WHO) launched its '3 by 5' strategy. This aims to give three million people in developing countries access to anti-retrovirals (ARVs) by 2005, two million of whom are supposed to be in Africa. But implementation of this initiative has been extremely slow. At present, a mere 50,000 Africans are receiving ARVs (*ibid*).

Without much more decisive action and a major increase in access to ARVs and other treatments, millions more Africans will die from the disease. Two million Africans died of AIDS in 2003 alone, while fifteen million have died on the continent over the last two decades. African women are disproportionately affected, with thirteen infected women for every ten infected men. Twelve million African children have been orphaned by HIV/AIDS, and it is estimated that in 2010, over eighteen million children will have lost one or both parents (UNICEF, 2005). The number of double orphans – children whose mother and father have both died – will increase by about two million over the same period. Millions more are living in households with sick or dying family members.

HIV/AIDS is drastically reducing life expectancy levels across Africa. In Botswana, for example, life expectancy has fallen from sixty-five in 1990 to below thirty-five today, while in Swaziland it has dropped from fifty-five in the 1980s to around thirty. In some African countries, around sixty per cent of fifteen year olds are unlikely to live to old age as a consequence of the disease (UNAIDS, 2004). By 2010, life expectancy in some African countries could be lower than at the start of the twentieth century (Gordon, 2001).

These statistics – horrifying as they are – barely begin to convey the scale of the human suffering involved for millions of Africans. It is also clear that the worst is yet to come. The pandemic has very far from reached its peak, with infection rates still outstripping deaths from AIDS in most African nations. The US National Intelligence Council has talked about 'the next wave' of HIV/AIDS. It predicts that in Nigeria, Africa's most populous country, the number of infected people may reach fifteen million by 2010, and that in Ethiopia infections may reach ten million by the same date (US National Intelligence Council, 2002).

The disease can also spread extremely quickly, unless preventative steps are taken. Prevalence in Swaziland, for example, has jumped from four to forty per cent in the course of a decade (AAPPG, 2004). In many other parts of Africa – Angola, the DRC and Sudan – the full extent of the epidemic is not yet known. The very uniqueness of the HIV/AIDS crisis means that there are no models for dealing with it, and the impact of the disease further weakens the capacity of societies to counter it.

The best estimates of epidemiologists are that the HIV/AIDS epidemic will last for more than a century. Some suspect that this is an optimistic prediction, because it overlooks the vicious cycle whereby AIDS contributes to poverty and distress, the very factors that render the next generation more vulnerable to HIV. Yes, AIDS is an emergency, demanding an immediate response. But no, we cannot expect this emergency to be over in our lifetimes and 'normal development' to resume. (de Waal, 2004)

HIV/AIDS is having, and will have, huge and unparalleled implications for the economy, politics and security of African states (Amoako, 2003). HIV/AIDS is impacting very severely on the livelihoods and food security of African families and communities. The disease means a loss of income, as well as the loss of labour of the person who falls ill. It involves increased expenditure on medicines. Invariably other family members will miss school or work to care for the patient. Where individuals die from AIDS this means a permanent loss of income and often the removal of children from school, damaging future earnings potential. Where both parents die, the cost of bringing up orphaned children is passed to other relatives (UNAIDS, 2004; Barnett and Whiteside, 2002). However, in numerous cases, traditional family structures and coping mechanisms are breaking down, with children left without any care and support. The consequences for social cohesion are only beginning to become apparent, with evidence from southern Africa that AIDS orphans are disproportionately likely to become involved in crime (Barnett and Whiteside, 2002).

At the macro level, HIV/AIDS is damaging the economy of many African countries. This occurs through additional costs on businesses due to employee sickness and insurance, absenteeism and the human capital costs of training replacement staff (AAPPG, 2004). The World Bank has estimated that HIV/AIDS already costs Africa 0.8 per cent of economic growth per year. The same report estimated that in a country with twenty per cent HIV prevalence the likely loss to annual GDP growth would be around 2.6 per cent. Over a twenty-year period GDP would actually be sixty-seven per cent less than without HIV/AIDS, a massive loss of income in already desperately poor countries (*ibid*).

HIV/AIDS is also having an impact on the provision of health and education services. Huge numbers of African teachers, nurses, doctors and associated staff have died or become ill from HIV/AIDS. In South Africa alone, between 80,000 and 133,000 teachers will have died from AIDS-related illnesses by 2010 (Bermejo, 2004). It is estimated that the Zambian health system lost twenty-five per cent of its professional staff in 2003, of which one-third was due to AIDS; while in Malawi up to seventy per cent of hospital beds are occupied by patients suffering from AIDS-related illnesses (Elbe, 2003).

HIV/AIDS is also likely to undermine the capacity of many African states to govern effectively and could seriously destabilise already fragile states. There are five specific ways in which this could happen. First, HIV/AIDS will divert resources from the provision of state services to the treatment of those infected. Services will also become increasingly difficult to deliver with higher mortality rates linked to HIV/AIDS. For example, between 1998 and 2000, AIDS caused seventy-five per cent of the deaths in the Kenyan police force, severely reducing the capacity of the force to combat crime in the country (The Nation, 2000). Second, HIV/AIDS could 'reconfigure political power' in a country with high prevalence rates (Elbe, 2003). Elbe also suggests that tensions could particularly arise 'if one group felt itself to be disproportionately affected, and believed that other groups were deliberately not doing enough to address the issue'. Third, HIV/AIDS could generate political tensions over access to drugs for treating the disease, for example if ARVs were available to one group but not to another. Fourth, HIV/AIDS could seriously weaken the military and security forces within a country. Some of Africa's armies have infection rates as high as sixty per cent. In already fragile African states the perception of a weakened security apparatus could invite opposition groups to instigate civil unrest or worse (Institute for Security Studies, 2003). Fifth, HIV/AIDS orphans are likely to be easily recruited into child soldiering. HIV/AIDS therefore poses severe threats to political stability and security in many African societies.

The responsibilities of the G8

HIV/AIDS and other issues such as endemic poverty and widespread conflict, are not problems that African governments can solve alone. They therefore raise critical questions about the obligations of those outside Africa. If African governments and people must take more responsibility for the state of their continent, so too must the governments of rich countries, including the G8. Too often, Africa's development plight is seen as an exclusively internal phenomenon in need of an external remedy. Yet some of the policies currently pursued by G8 countries are actually damaging Africa. Other G8 policies are hindering rather than helping Africa to achieve more capable states, better governance and greater progress in development. These 'harmful' G8 policies are the specific subject of this ippr report.

It is worth briefly explaining the reasons for this chosen focus. There are of course many things that Africans themselves must do to improve the prospects for their continent. This is accepted by the governments that have signed up to NEPAD, and by the AU, the UN Economic Commission for Africa, and many others within African governments, private sector and civil society. These bodies have already developed many ideas and policy proposals for better governance and improved economic performance in Africa. There are also many good things that G8 and other developed countries can do with and for Africa, for example strengthening Africa's capacity to manage conflict, providing resources to tackle HIV/AIDS and supporting African institutions such as the AU. This is a major focus of the work of the Commission for Africa, set up by the UK Government in 2004 and due to report in early 2005. However, the extent to which the existing policies of G8 countries may be damaging Africa is an area that still receives too little attention. But it is the area where G8 countries have least excuse for inaction and where the benefits of better policy could be most far-reaching.

G8 countries are critical players in their own right, but they also have significant influence over regional bodies such as the EU and international financial institutions such as the World Bank and the International Monetary Fund (IMF). As an absolute priority, G8 countries should 'put their own house in order' and end those policies that stymie Africa's development. Greater political will on the part of G8 governments can help to secure the necessary changes in policy. But this is much more likely to occur if there is sustained and vigorous public pressure on G8 governments to act differently, and if G8 governments are held properly and publicly to account for their policies towards Africa, particularly in relation to coherence issues.

The opportunity of 2005

G8 countries have a clear moral responsibility to change those policies that leave Africa disadvantaged. But it is also in their interests to do so. The consequences of Africa's poverty will not remain confined within Africa's borders. Poverty and underdevelopment create fertile conditions for a new set of security threats, including violent conflict, crime and terrorism, the spread of disease, and the trafficking of people, arms and illicit drugs. A more stable, prosperous and democratic Africa would also bring enormous benefits, opening up opportunities for mutually beneficial trade, investment and cultural exchange and the more effective management of common problems.

As the opening quotation from Gordon Brown makes clear, 2005 represents a critical year of opportunity for Africa. The creation of NEPAD and the AU suggests a new willingness within many parts of Africa to reform political systems, economies and societies. G8 countries have also indicated a willingness to do more to develop a stronger partnership with Africa. The Commission for Africa, the UK's forthcoming presidencies of the EU and the G8, and the September UN review conference on progress towards the MDGs all create opportunities for substantive progress on issues that matter to Africa.

The structure of the report

This report focuses on five specific areas.

Chapter 1 looks at aid and conditionality. It considers the way that aid is currently used by G8 countries in Africa, including the practice of tied aid and the various costs and distortions imposed on African societies by bad donor policies. It also examines debt relief and the implications of donor conditionality and the policies of the IFIs for governance and political accountability in Africa.

Chapter 2 looks at trade and the way that the rules and practices of international trade work against Africa's interests. It considers G8 double standards on agricultural subsidies, including on specific products such as cotton and sugar. It examines the issue of market access for African exporters. The chapter also looks at the implications of intellectual property rules for Africa and at how Africa's interests might be better safeguarded in the international trading system, including through the proposed EPAs between the EU and the ACP countries, and through Special and Differential Treatment provisions.

Chapter 3 focuses on arms proliferation. It assesses the role played by arms proliferation in fuelling and exacerbating conflict on the continent, considers direct exports by G8 countries to African governments and rebel groups, and looks at the role of G8 arms brokers, traffickers and transport agents.

Chapter 4 considers corruption and conflict financing. It assesses the involvement of G8 companies in corruption in Africa, and the various measures adopted by G8 and other governments to help counter it. The chapter also considers several initiatives that have been taken to deal with the financing of violent conflict in Africa through better regulation of the trade in commodities such as oil, diamonds and timber.

Chapter 5 addresses climate change. It considers the likely impacts of climate change on Africa and the contribution made by G8 countries to this process. It examines several ways by which G8 countries could clean up their act, through agreements to lower emissions, supporting renewable sources of energy, endorsing a more equitable framework for emissions and strengthening Africa's capacity to adapt to climate change.

On all these issues – aid and conditionality, trade, arms transfers, corruption and conflict financing and climate change – G8 countries need to put their own house in order if Africa is to make greater development progress and to stand any chance of achieving the MDGs.

The **Conclusion** considers how G8 countries can promote more coherent policies towards Africa and be better held to account for the impact of these policies.

1 Rethinking aid and conditionality

Better aid means that we must match our priorities with those of African states. As donors, we must get our act together, and not impose too great an administrative burden on those to whom we give or loan our money.

Hilary Benn, UK Secretary of State for International Development
(6 December, 2004)

If Africa is to make greater progress towards the achievement of the MDGs, it will require significantly increased aid resources from the G8 and other rich countries. While it is critically important for Africa to attract greater private investment and to boost levels of economic growth, many of the poorest African countries are going to remain dependent on aid flows in the short to medium term, not least to meet the huge additional costs posed by the HIV/AIDS pandemic. The WHO has suggested that an extra seven billion dollars a year is needed to provide life-sustaining anti-retroviral treatment (ARV) to the millions of Africans living with HIV and AIDS (de Waal, 2004). This figure is almost certainly an underestimate; it does not include, for example, the costs of nutrition, shelter and clean water, which people with HIV and AIDS need if they are to benefit from treatment. The figure is also likely to grow, as more people come forward for treatment and as more people become infected. But seven billion dollars represents about half of what Africa currently receives in international aid. Large additional investments are also needed to tackle illiteracy and ill-health, and for improvements in agriculture, infrastructure and the provision of clean water and sanitation (Sachs *et al.*, 2004).

But increased aid resources – while vital – need to be provided in new ways, if they are to help rather than hinder the achievement of more capable African states and more effective development on the continent. Too often in the past, and too frequently still, the impact of aid is much less than its potential. In some countries this is because aid has been misused by recipient governments, expropriated by Africa's elites at the expense of Africa's poor (van de Walle, 2001). But it is also because G8 countries – and the IFIs that they largely control – have often allocated aid in accordance with narrow strategic, commercial or political interests rather than focusing it on the goal of poverty reduction, or because aid has been spent in the wrong countries, on the wrong things and in the wrong ways.

High levels of debt owed to G8 countries and the IFIs – and often incurred on their advice – also divert resources in many African countries from pressing development priorities and stymie progress towards the

MDGs. Debt relief is a form of aid and is subject to many of the same types of conditionalities as traditional aid. In various other ways inappropriate donor policies can damage or disadvantage Africa, imposing heavy transaction costs on recipient countries and weakening the capacity of African governments. At its worst, aid transfers and inappropriate donor conditionality produce a form of external dependency and weaken systems of domestic accountability. If aid to Africa is to be part of the solution, rather than part of the problem, this needs to change radically.

Improving the effectiveness of development aid

Increasing development aid and focusing it on the poorest

Despite the scale of Africa's needs and the worsening of the continent's overall development indicators, none of the G8 countries currently meets the UN 0.7 per cent aid/GNP target, and only two countries – the UK and France – have set deadlines for reaching it. On current rates of progress, Canada will not reach the target until 2025, the US until 2040, Germany until 2087 and Italy until 2111. Japan, meanwhile, is cutting its aid budget, and therefore moving even further from the UN target.

Of the G8 countries, the UK has been the most vocal in making the case for a big increase in international aid resources. The UK Chancellor, Gordon Brown, has put forward a proposal for an IFF, a way of leveraging additional resources from the international capital markets by securing binding future commitments from aid donors (HM Treasury, 2004).

But while the overall level of G8 aid spending is important, so too is the way that aid is allocated, both between countries and within them. Some G8 donors still allocate a disproportionate amount of aid to high or middle income rather than low income countries. For example, two of the top recipients of French aid – French Polynesia and New Caledonia – and Israel, one of the top recipients of US aid, are classified as high income countries (Oxfam, 2004). Since 11 September 2001, there is also a growing concern that more aid will be allocated according to donors' strategic interests, and less in response to poor people's needs. For example, there is some evidence that the US is providing more aid to countries seen as important to or supportive of 'the war on terror', even when those countries have a weak commitment to tackling poverty and have poor records on human rights (*ibid*). Poor people in Africa are likely to lose out from these new donor priorities.

Ending tied aid

The quality of the aid provided by some G8 countries is severely weakened by the practice of aid tying. Tied aid – making aid dependent on the purchase of goods and services from the donor country – distorts and damages development in three significant ways. Firstly, it reduces the value of aid by an estimated twenty-five per cent, depriving African countries of resources that could be used elsewhere (DFID, 2000). Secondly, it promotes gross inefficiency, with countries being supplied with incompatible pieces of equipment by different development donors, each with separate requirements for spares and back-up. Take the case of an African country wanting to reform its health sector. Rather than procuring the most cost-effective supplies available, tied aid forces the country to divide up procurement to fit the separate and differing requirements of several development donors. Thirdly, it hinders the growth of domestic industries in the recipient country as supplies are not sourced locally. Tied aid is therefore wholly inconsistent with the idea of African-owned and African-led development, as set out by NEPAD and the AU.

In 2001, the OECD countries – including the G8 – agreed to untie their aid to Least Developed Countries (LDCs) (the majority of which are African) 'to the greatest extent possible' (the so-called Development Assistance Committee (DAC) Recommendation). The agreement came into force on 1 January 2002. The DAC recommendation was also reaffirmed at the Financing for Development Conference in Monterrey in 2002. While there has been some progress on untying, G8 countries, including the US, Italy and France, have been prominent amongst those that have dragged their feet on implementing the Recommendation (ActionAid, 2003).

The 2001 DAC Recommendation also contains a number of important exclusions that have significantly limited its impact (DAC, 2004). For example, food aid and technical cooperation are exempt from its provisions, although they represent a large proportion of aid (*ibid*). Tied food aid encourages the provision of donor country food supplies even when locally available food could be provided more cheaply and efficiently. Making African and other poor countries dependent on imported food supplies undermines local producers and increases countries' vulnerability to food shortages and famine. Tied technical assistance imposes particular costs on Africa. According to a World Bank report 'some 100,000 foreign technical experts are currently employed in Africa, tending to displace local experts' (Dollar, 2001).

Avoiding donor duplication and supporting national capacity

Tied aid is just one example – although a particularly egregious one – of the way in which bad donor policy can distort and damage Africa's development prospects. More broadly, however, the policies of G8 and other donors towards Africa are often badly coordinated, impose high transaction costs on recipient countries and can weaken rather than strengthen African state capacity. While Africa has put a mechanism in place in the form of NEPAD to coordinate its relationship with the donor community, this has not been reciprocated by G8 countries. The G8 does not have a secretariat and G8 countries are still far from being coherent and coordinated in their policies towards Africa.

Too often, African countries face a range of different development donors, each pushing their own agenda, and each with their own different and burdensome reporting requirements. To give one example, in 2002–3 the government of Tanzania received a staggering 275 separate donor missions, 123 from the World Bank alone, demanding time-consuming attention from Tanzania's scarce government and administrative personnel (Oxfam, 2004).

The problem of bad donor policy and poor coordination can be illustrated clearly with reference to HIV/AIDS. Development aid for responding to Africa's HIV/AIDS crisis comes in a wide variety of forms. Recent initiatives and sources of funding include the World Bank's Multi-Country HIV/AIDS Program (MAP) for Africa, launched in 2000; the Global Fund to Fight AIDS, Tuberculosis and Malaria, launched in 2002; and the US President's Emergency Plan for AIDS relief (PEPFAR), launched in January 2003. These initiatives are in addition to many other bilateral and multilateral programmes, as well as the work of private foundations and companies. The sheer number of different funding streams and initiatives causes serious difficulties for Africa.

> Donor ambitions and frequent changes in international financing mechanisms are absorbing much needed human capacity in Africa. A case study of Kenya shows that the Ministry of Health has profoundly changed its role from being focused on policy-making, planning and quality assurance to one of resource mobilisation and managing multiple relationships with donors ... An increasingly complex web of donors and funding routes has emerged and there is no mechanism to prevent duplication of effort. (Bermejo, 2004)

In response to these proliferating initiatives and funds and the problems they cause for Africa, some important steps have been taken to try to promote greater donor coordination. In April 2004, the Joint United Nations Programme on HIV/AIDS (UNAIDS) launched a set of principles called the 'Three Ones'. The Three Ones approach calls for the adoption of a single national HIV/AIDS coordinating body, a single national action framework on HIV/AIDS and a single monitoring and evaluation framework. While key donors, including from the G8, have endorsed this approach, implementation has been poor. Civil society groups are an important part of the response to the pandemic, but are not included in the Three Ones framework as it is currently structured. This needs to change. However, it is also essential that G8 countries minimise the costs they impose on African societies that are struggling to deal with HIV/AIDS.

Donors need to change the way they relate to Africa, both on HIV/AIDS and more broadly. In February 2003, the World Bank and the major bilateral aid donors, including the G8, committed themselves to the Rome Declaration. This called on donors to deliver aid in accordance with the priorities of the recipient country and adopt common procedures for delivering aid, reduce the numbers of missions, reports and conditions, be more transparent, and provide more predictable levels of aid funding (Rome Declaration, 2003). To date, most G8 countries have not done nearly enough to implement the provisions of this Declaration.

In the right circumstances, donors can also use aid more effectively in Africa through Poverty Reduction Budget Support (PRBS). This can take two main forms: either a general contribution to the overall budget, often described as General Budget Support (GBS), or financial aid earmarked for a particular sector, usually described as Sector Budget Support (SBS). While donors need to be confident that the potential recipients of budget support will use the resources well, PRBS can be an important means for strengthening the capacity of African systems and the effectiveness of aid (DFID, 2004).

G8 countries should:

- Commit to reaching the UN 0.7 per cent aid/national income target by 2010 and set up the IFF as soon as possible.

- Substantially increase funding for tackling HIV/AIDS to: help improve access to prevention, care and treatment services, including a huge increase in the provision of anti-retrovirals; support the strengthening of African healthcare systems and civil society groups working to combat the disease; and provide donor support in line with the 'Three Ones' principles.

- Untie all bilateral aid to all African countries, simplify reporting requirements and implement the Rome Declaration on good donor practice, including more predictable levels of aid funding.

Reducing the burden of debt

Despite some significant progress over recent years, many African countries are still suffering from high and unsustainable levels of external debt. This debt burden – sometimes incurred by following poor advice from IFIs – continues to be an obstacle to reducing poverty and the achievement of more capable states in Africa.

Under the Heavily Indebted Poor Countries (HIPC) initiative, first launched in 1996, African and other heavily indebted poor countries were supposed to see cuts in debt payments and reductions in debt to 'sustainable' levels. HIPC has produced substantial debt relief for some African countries, for example, twelve African countries have reached their HIPC Completion Point – the point at which debt relief becomes irrevocable – and these countries have received around twenty-six billion dollars in HIPC debt relief (Jubilee, 2004). Debt payments in African HIPC countries are also down from taking an average of nearly thirty per cent of government revenues to eleven per cent, with nearly sixty-five per cent of these savings now being spent on health and education (Brown, 2004). But in other African countries, annual debt service payments continue at high levels. For instance, in 2003 Senegal spent almost thirty-six per cent of its revenues on debt service and Malawi paid around thirty per cent (IDA/IMF, 2004).

Moreover, eight years on from the launch of HIPC, only four African countries have seen their debt burdens cut to 'sustainable' levels (*ibid*). In large part this is a consequence of many African countries' declining export revenues (HIPC sustainability levels are defined as within 150 per cent of their annual exports), and by the excessively narrow criteria of HIPC. In some cases, debt burdens are well above this level. For example, Uganda has a debt amounting to more than 250 per cent of exports, while Ethiopia's debt burden will remain at over 200 per cent of its exports until at least 2010, despite so-called 'topping up' at the HIPC Completion Point (*ibid*). Bringing about real sustainability will require additional resources and/or a change in the sustainability criteria.

While the large bilateral creditors, including the G8 countries, have in the main agreed to cancel the debts owed to them by African and other poor countries, significant levels of debt continue to be owed by Africa to the multilateral institutions, such as the World Bank, the IMF and the African Development Bank. The first two institutions' policies are, of course, largely shaped by the G8 countries. Reducing these debts will require additional resources, either from G8 donors or from the institutions themselves. The UK has already agreed to pay its share of the debt service owed by low-income countries to the World Bank and the African Development Bank. While this is a welcome initiative, it will require other G8 countries' involvement to be effective and should be in addition to current aid budgets. Another proposal would be to use some of the IMF's gold stocks, something supported by the UK Government. It has been estimated that gold revaluation could potentially raise more than thirty billion dollars to fund debt relief (Kapoor, 2004). This would help fund the IMF's share of multilateral debt relief, and possibly also that of the World Bank and the other multilateral creditors. IMF gold was sold previously – in 1999–2000 – to help fund debt relief for Mexico and Brazil. This was carried out successfully, without any adverse effects on the financial credit worthiness of the IFIs (*ibid*).

G8 countries should:

- Support one hundred per cent multilateral debt cancellation for all low-income African countries that demonstrate that they will use the proceeds to benefit the poor, with debt relief financed by either additional donor contributions or the sale or revaluation of IMF gold.

- Replace the current debt sustainability framework with one that links debt relief to the resources needed by countries to meet the MDGs.

Preventing aid from weakening African state capacity also requires new thinking on conditionality. Conditionality is defined here as the terms and conditions that must be met by recipients before donors will provide aid resources. Conditions are placed on aid by both bilateral aid donors, including the G8, and by the IFIs, such as the World Bank and the IMF. Indeed, the IMF has a particularly important role in respect of conditionality, acting as the effective 'gate keeper' for poor countries' access to aid resources. The IMF's view of a country's economic performance is frequently decisive in terms of the position taken by bilateral donors. But it often adopts a highly conservative and short-term approach to economic reform issues that limits and distorts Africa's development options, for example by pushing for reductions in public expenditure even when countries have a stable macro-economic framework and have huge unmet development and humanitarian needs to respond to.

This is a massive issue when it comes to HIV/AIDS. The IFIs are still failing to face up to the scale of the HIV/AIDS pandemic and to rethink their approach to fiscal stability in countries where the disease is rampant. It cannot be right that the purchase of labour saving devices counts as productive expenditure, while life-saving measures are classified as non-productive. Moreover, pushing excessively restrictive budgetary ceilings on governments and insisting on the downsizing of bureaucracies can hinder African responses to the pandemic. Addressing the HIV/AIDS crisis requires a 'social protection package' on a huge scale, and this just 'isn't compatible with macro-economic frameworks that focus on fiscal stability to the exclusion of all else... The basis for macro-economic stability must be the resilience of the social fabric; the foundation of fiscal responsibility must be human security' (de Waal, 2004).

In recent years, traditional donor conditionality has been subject to additional criticisms. Three in particular stand out. Firstly, traditional conditionality is seen to have been relatively ineffective. This may be because governments have declined to carry out the policies that donors required of them or that donors have carried on providing aid even though these conditions were not being met, or that the conditions were unrealistic (Killick, 1998; 2002). Secondly, traditional conditionality is seen as seriously weakening domestic political accountability, with Africa's governments more accountable to their aid donors than to their own people (de Waal, 2004). Thirdly, there is a concern that conditionality has sometimes been used to push policies on African countries that have been damaging to the poor, for example privatisation of public utilities or trade and investment liberalisation (ActionAid, 2004; War on Want/PCS, 2004).

There is important truth in some of these criticisms. Heavy-handed conditionality is invariably ineffective. As the UK Government puts it, 'conditionality that attempts to buy reform from an unwilling partner has rarely worked' (DFID/HM Treasury/FCO, 2004). Moreover, conditionality has often weakened the accountability of Africa's governments and undermined national political processes. Dogmatic or heavy-handed policy conditionality can also damage Africa. Privatisation or trade liberalisation are not necessarily bad for the poor (the record is mixed and a lot depends on how it is done), but there are clear cases in which its effects have been negative (ActionAid, 2004). It is certainly inappropriate to attempt to foist such policies on African countries when they are not supported by these governments, without any assessment of their impact on the poor or without consultation with affected groups.

G8 countries can also push their ideological prejudices through aid conditionality. Take the US Administration and its approach to the funding of HIV/AIDS programmes. Within PEPFAR, one-third of US prevention funding is reserved for 'abstinence only' programmes. While abstinence might be appropriate behaviour for some people, making it a condition for supporting HIV/AIDS programmes in Africa has seriously negative consequences, particularly for African women. As the International HIV/AIDS Alliance has argued:

> Many women who have taken the route of abstinence until marriage, and have remained faithful inside marriage, have become infected by their husbands. And in many of these countries, women are simply not able to negotiate using condoms within marriage. (Bermejo, 2004)

A policy that makes funding for HIV/AIDS conditional on promoting abstinence is penalising some of Africa's poorest women and making it much harder to tackle the disease. The US has also used conditionality to push countries to sign bilateral agreements that they won't hand over US soldiers to the International Criminal Court. This is a complete misuse of development conditionality.

Over the last decade, there have been a number of important changes in thinking around development policy that have impacted on the conditionality debate. There has been a growing consensus, for example, around the primacy of poverty reduction as the goal of development cooperation, and the importance of national ownership of countries' development strategies and popular participation in putting these strategies together. This is central to the idea of Poverty Reduction Strategy Papers (PRSPs). However, there is concern that the PRSP process is still falling well short of this ideal. For example, IMF and World Bank processes such as Poverty Reduction and Growth Facility negotiations and the Country Policy and Institutional Assessments often continue to take precedence over the PRSP process (CIDSE and Caritas Internationalis, 2004).

At the same time, there has been a demand for greater openness and mutual accountability between donors and recipients, and for more focus on issues around human rights (which might imply rather more conditionality in some respects) (Mepham and Cooper, 2004). Aid to states with poor human rights records or very poor standards of governance obviously raises difficult issues. In general, it is important to stay engaged with such countries, to use whatever leverage exists to help promote reform, better governance and greater observance of human rights. But there will clearly be circumstances in which it is not appropriate to provide direct government to government aid, particularly if this might strengthen a repressive government or if the resources would be misused. Memoranda of Understanding – setting out the respective responsibilities of donors and recipients – could help to clarify the circumstances in which aid to governments would be withdrawn. It is also important to continue to provide assistance to poor people living in these countries. Sometimes this can be done by working with particular ministries or regional or local government. Civil society groups can be an important way of reaching those in need as they are often best placed to deliver aid at the community level. Developed countries, including the G8, need to think more coherently and imaginatively about how they provide assistance in such fragile states (DFID, 2005).

G8 governments should:

- Promote a new approach to conditionality, linked to African governments' own development goals and their PRSs: these goals should be openly debated, above all within African countries themselves, including within Africa's parliaments and with civil society.

- Promote a less rigid and more balanced approach to macro-economic stability within the IFIs, especially the IMF, with IFI support linked to countries' PRSs.

- Not attempt to foist controversial policies on African countries, for example utility privatisation: it is for African countries to decide whether these policies are beneficial or not, preferably following a full Poverty and Social Impact Analysis (PSIA) and consultation with the communities likely to be affected.

- Be clearer about the circumstances in which aid would be reduced or withdrawn from governments: relevant criteria should include countries' compliance with international obligations on human rights and peace and security, and these circumstances should be specified in Memoranda of Understanding between donors and African partners.

- Promote 'process conditions', for example ones that increase transparency and strengthen the participation of poor people in decision-making, although these should be designed carefully so as not to undermine national political processes.

2 Supporting fairer global rules of trade

We commit to providing greater market access for African products – including by applying our Doha commitment to comprehensive negotiations on agriculture aimed at substantial improvements in market access, reductions of all forms of export subsidies with a view to their being phased out, and substantial reductions in trade-distorting domestic support.

G8 Africa Action Plan (27 June, 2002)

While international trade could potentially bring huge benefits to Africa, global trade rules and the existing policies of G8 countries are severely damaging Africa's development prospects and worsening the living conditions and life chances of many of its people. If Africa could increase its share of world exports by just one per cent this would generate an additional $70 billion worth of income – around five times the amount it currently receives through aid and debt relief (Benn, 2004). But far from Africa increasing its proportion of world trade, over the last two decades this share has fallen dramatically. It currently accounts for less than two per cent of global exports – around a third of its share at the start of the 1980s (DTI, 2004). The development consequences of these deteriorating trade figures have been disastrous. Falling export revenues in many African countries have weakened state capacity and reduced the resources available for tackling ill-health, HIV/AIDS, illiteracy, poor sanitation and income poverty. It has been estimated that if sub-Saharan Africa had retained the same share of world exports as it had in 1980, the average per capita income across the continent would be roughly double what it is today (Oxfam, 2002a).

There are various complex reasons for this decline. These include a range of 'supply side' constraints within African societies themselves, such as poor health and levels of education, skills and productivity, poor governance, and weaknesses in transport, customs and communications infrastructure. Collectively these factors seriously limit the extent to which African countries can take advantage of trading opportunities when these arise. But the gross unfairness of G8 countries' trade policies is another critical part of the explanation and an important contributory cause of Africa's continuing poverty and marginalisation in the global economy. Across a range of issues, the policies of G8 countries are hindering rather than helping Africa to capture the benefits from international trade.

The Doha international trade meeting in 2001 called for a new multilateral trade round to be a 'development round'. For almost two and a half years negotiations were deadlocked, not least because of the unwillingness of the world's richer countries to make basic concessions on agriculture. However, in July 2004, a breakthrough of sorts occurred at a World Trade Organisation (WTO) meeting in Geneva with the conclusion of a framework agreement. It is essential to seize the opportunity afforded by the resumption of these negotiations to promote a new approach to international trade, one that brings real benefits to Africa and other poorer parts of the world.

In making the case for reform, it is important to highlight that the costs of existing policies are not confined to Africa. G8 consumers and taxpayers also lose out from subsidies imposed at the behest of vested agricultural interests. For example, EU taxpayers pay for the Common Agricultural Policy (CAP) budget, which stood at €45 billion in 2002 (Thurston, 2002). The total annual cost to EU consumers of artificially high food prices is estimated to be in the region of €50 billion (*ibid*). This regime is benefiting a handful of farmers in the EU but is destroying the livelihoods of many farmers in Africa and raising food prices for EU consumers. The G8 is an important forum in which to highlight these costs and to mobilise pressure for win-win policy reforms.

Ending G8 double standards on agricultural subsidies

Agriculture provides two-thirds of Africa's employment, half of its exports and over one-third of its Gross National Income (DTI, 2004). Fairer international trade in agriculture would therefore be of particular benefit to Africa. But despite their free market rhetoric, most G8 countries provide very substantial subsidies for their agricultural sectors. These subsidies are enormously damaging to Africa and other poorer parts of the world. They depress world market prices of agricultural products by encouraging overproduction. They increase the volatility of agriculture prices and disadvantage African producers in their own and third country markets. And they can force small-scale African farmers out of business. This occurs at the same time that IFIs often insist that African governments cut price support and subsidies for their own farmers.

The worst culprits when it comes to agricultural subsidies are the EU countries and the US. In 2002, support to agricultural producers in these countries was an estimated $250 billion – about five times the level of global development aid (*ibid*). The EU countries have made some recent steps towards the reform of the grossly inefficient CAP, including a reduction in agricultural export subsidies, although there is still much further to go. Agricultural interests, particularly in France, continue to be a powerful obstacle to further CAP reform. In the US, the 2002 Farm Bill has led to a significant increase in agricultural subsidies, with expenditure on agriculture set to increase by eighty-three billion dollars over the next ten years (*ibid*).

The adverse consequences of G8 agricultural subsidies, and the unfairness of existing international trade rules, can be illustrated with reference to cotton and West Africa. In Benin, Burkina Faso, Chad, Mali and Togo more than ten million people depend on cotton for their livelihoods. Cotton accounts for five to ten per cent of GDP, more than one-third of total export receipts and over two-thirds of the value of agricultural exports (Gillson, 2004). But these countries face a heavily depressed cotton market and declining export earnings caused, in part, by G8 subsidies.

The US provides four billion dollars in subsidies to its cotton sector. This is nearly twice what it gives in development aid to the whole of sub-Saharan Africa, and more than the combined GDP of the main cotton-producing countries in West Africa (Oxfam, 2004a). The EU provides a lower overall level of subsidy to its cotton producers. But EU subsidies are also highly damaging to West and Central African countries, with the subsidies received per unit of cotton by some European producers amongst the highest in the world (ODI, 2004).

G8 cotton subsidies are not just cutting export revenues in West Africa; they are also worsening levels of poverty. A study of the effects of cotton subsidies on Benin found that a forty per cent reduction in farm-level cotton prices led to a twenty-one per cent reduction in income for cotton farmers and a six to seven per cent increase in rural poverty (Minot and Daniels, 2002).

The unfairness of cotton subsidies and the way in which they have been used by G8 countries has not gone unchallenged. This was raised by a number of West and Central African countries at the Cancun trade talks in 2003, which subsequently collapsed, in part as a result of this issue (Tibaijuka, 2004). Cotton subsidies also formed the basis of a WTO Dispute brought by Brazil against the US in which it was ruled, on 26 April 2004, in favour of Brazil. The WTO stated that US policy towards cotton violated commitments to reduce subsidies. In the WTO meeting in Geneva in July 2004, governments agreed to introduce cotton subsidy reforms but did not set a timetable for action.

Agricultural subsides are also a big problem when it comes to sugar. Each year, Europe – a high-cost producer – 'generates an export surplus of approximately five million tonnes of sugar. This surplus is dumped overseas through a system of direct and indirect export subsidies, destroying markets for more efficient developing country producers in the process' (Oxfam, 2004b).

African countries are amongst the biggest losers from EU sugar policy. South Africa, for example, lost an estimated sixty million dollars in foreign exchange in 2002 (*ibid*). African sugar producers also suffer because of restricted market access to the EU (an issue addressed in the following section).

G8 countries should:

- Phase out all agricultural export subsidies.

- Eliminate all trade-distorting cotton subsidies by the time of the Hong Kong WTO Ministerial conference in December 2005 and provide, as an interim measure, financial compensation to African countries that are affected adversely by these subsidies.

- Reform fundamentally their support for the sugar sector: for the EU, there is a particular opportunity to do this in the context of the ongoing review of the CAP sugar regime.

Improving market access for African exporters

Many African countries have preferential market access with G8 countries. In the case of the EU, forty-four African countries have fairly good market access arrangements under the Cotonou Agreement and thirty-three African LDCs have preferential trade access under the Everything But Arms (EBA) initiative. The Canadian and Japanese Generalised System of Preferences (GSPs) apply to all developing countries and both have enhanced access for LDCs. The US' Africa Growth and Opportunity Act (AGOA) also provides thirty-eight African countries with preferential trade access to the US market. However, there are some important exceptions and qualifications to these various initiatives that continue to place serious obstacles in the way of African exporters.

Sugar is a clear example of developed countries' double standards on trade. Countries in the ACP group get preferential access to the European sugar market at prices linked to EU guaranteed prices. LDCs also have preferential market access. However, the EBA arrangements only allow African and other LDCs to export a tiny proportion of total EU sugar consumption (a mere one per cent). These EU market restrictions are especially costly for Ethiopia, Mozambique and Malawi, with the three countries losing an estimated $238 million since the introduction of the EBA in 2001 (Oxfam, 2004b). For every three dollars that the EU gives Mozambique in aid, it takes back one dollar through restrictions on access to its sugar market, and these export losses undermine investment and the scope for economic diversification (*ibid*).

Another problem facing African exporters is that of tariff escalation, whereby richer countries impose higher tariffs on processed imports than on unprocessed raw materials from the developing world. This restricts the ability of African countries to produce higher value-added products. For example, Ghana faces much higher EU tariffs on processed chocolate than on unprocessed cocoa butter or cocoa powder (Benn, 2004). A similar pattern is evident in the US. The US tariff on cocoa beans is zero per cent, rising to 0.2 per cent for semi-processed cocoa, and fifteen per cent on the final 'processed' product (DTI, 2004).

These G8 trade barriers have the effect of leaving many African countries heavily dependent on the export of primary commodities. These commodity prices are enormously volatile and have fallen significantly in value over the past thirty years. And the losses that result from falling commodity revenues are often greater than the value of aid and debt relief to individual African countries. The UN has estimated that for every dollar received by Africa since the early 1970s, fifty cents has been lost as a result of deteriorating terms of trade (*ibid*). Some modest steps have been taken to address the problem of primary commodity dependency. For example, the EU has launched an 'Action Plan on Commodities' and the United Nations Conference on Trade and Development (UNCTAD) has also sought to generate greater political interest in the issue. Overall, however, G8 and other developed countries have devoted remarkably little attention to an issue of pressing concern to many countries in Africa (Green, 2004).

African exporters are also hampered by 'rules of origin'. These specify when a product can be said to have been produced in a certain country. The rules are intended to ensure that the goods imported under a particular trade agreement were genuinely produced in the country in question. However, when rules of origin are applied too restrictively they can damage Africa's trading opportunities. For example, the export of tinned vegetables from Tanzania cannot benefit from the EU's EBA initiative if the tin cans come from a neighbouring country, thereby denying Tanzania a major potential source of export earnings. A similar issue has arisen in respect of Lesotho's clothing industry. While some clothing was exported to the EU in the 1980s and 1990s under an exemption from the rules of origin, from 1996 that exemption has been removed and Lesotho's clothing exports have fallen dramatically (Stevens and Kennan, 2004). Lesotho now exports twenty times less to the EU than to the US, largely because of the EU's excessively onerous rules of origin (Brenton and Ikezuki, 2004).

While the US AGOA has more relaxed rules (from which countries like Lesotho have benefited very significantly), it can be criticised for exempting large numbers of product lines of real potential benefit to Africa from its preferential market access terms. The AGOA still leaves 911 manufacturing product lines restricted out of a total of 8660. For the fourteen African LDCs that do not receive special clothing preferences, 1465 lines remain to be liberalised. This has a particularly negative impact on Africa's leather, textile and clothing sectors (*ibid*).

Africa's capacity to export can also be hindered by high product standards in G8 and other richer countries, especially the phytosanitary rules governing agricultural products. It has been estimated that the impact of changes in EU standards on aflatoxin levels in food would reduce the health risk to the EU by approximately 1.4 deaths in a billion, yet this rule reduced African exports of cereals, dried fruits and nuts by more than sixty per cent – a loss of $670 million (Benn, 2004). Consumers in G8 countries are understandably pressing for tighter hygiene and safety standards in respect of the food they eat. In response, governments in these countries are legislating to raise standards and putting in place processes to ensure that standards are enforced. However, African countries often find these standards – and those set by northern supermarket chains – hard to comply with. To prevent African countries being adversely affected by standards in G8 countries, they need to be able to participate more fully and meaning-fully in the scientific and policy discussions that establish these standards, and they need to be given time and technical assistance to meet G8 product standards. This is not happening at present (Stevens, 2003).

Some African countries will also be affected badly by reductions in trade barriers (*ibid*). For example, if developed countries such as the EU continue to lower barriers to imports (as a consequence of multilateral trade liberali-sation), this will have the effect of eroding the trade preferences enjoyed by the ACP countries under the Cotonou Agreement. The IMF has estimated that Malawi, Mauritania, Cape Verde and Sao Tome and Principe would suffer major losses in agriculture as a result (IMF, 2003). In response to these concerns, in March 2004 the IMF established the Trade Integration Mechanism, which will provide funding to those countries, based on expected losses from preference erosion (Page, 2004).

Special attention may also need to be given to the development prob-lems posed for Africa by the growth of China and India. China, in par-ticular, now dominates developing country exports of all types. Kenya and Lesotho will face growing competition from China and India in relation to clothing and apparel with the phase-out of the Multi-Fibre Arrangement for textiles trade. The longer-term challenge for African economies is to diversify, boost productivity and break into new markets. In the short term, however, African countries are likely to need transitional financial support to adjust to the sometimes drastic consequences of 'preference erosion'.

G8 countries should:

- End tariff escalation by lowering tariffs on processed and semi-processed goods.

- Introduce simple and liberal rules of origin, so that African countries can source their inputs from the most competitive suppliers (technically known as 'cumulation') and derive greater benefit from trade preferences.

- Ensure that regulations – for example, those dealing with food safety – do not damage Africa's opportunities to trade.

- Give much higher priority to the issue of dependence on primary com-modities and help African countries to reduce their dependence, including by providing support for economic diversification into the production of higher value goods.

- Provide transitional financial support to African countries that are seriously disadvantaged by the erosion of international trade preferences.

Reforming rules on intellectual property

Another critical area where G8 policy is damaging Africa relates to international rules on intellectual property, including the Agreement on Trade Related Aspects of Intellectual Property (TRIPS). Forced through by the US at the last moment as part of the Uruguay Trade Round in 1994, TRIPS requires countries to introduce minimum standards of intellectual property protection. Developed countries were obliged to introduce these new rules by 2000, while LDCs were given an extension until 2016.

While this extension is important for the poorest African countries, TRIPS will still have the effect of pushing up the price of technology and other key products for many African countries and will increase the technological divide between the world's rich and poor. As the independent Commission on Intellectual Property Rights stated in its report:

> The contemporary evidence suggests that, because developing countries are large net importers of technology from the developed world, the globalisation of intellectual property protection will result in very substantial additional net transfers from developing to developed countries. (CIPR, 2002)

It is not hard to see why this should be the case. Richer countries' companies account for about ninety-seven per cent of all the patents in the world and most patents provided in developing countries are for foreign companies (Oxfam, 2002a). In Africa, hardly any patent protection (0.02 per cent) is provided to domestic residents (World Bank, 2000). Payments to patent holders therefore constitute a net transfer of resources out of Africa – even when the products themselves have been sourced from Africa.

This chapter focuses on just one aspect of the TRIPS issue – its impact on Africa's access to drugs for treating HIV/AIDS and other diseases. While there are diverse obstacles to the improvement of poor people's health and to tackling HIV/AIDS, and while the price of some drugs has fallen dramatically in recent years, lack of access to affordable medicines remains a critical issue in many parts of Africa. For example, the WTO estimates that the price for certain combinations of anti-retrovirals is $300 per person per year. However, in 2003 the governments of twenty-nine countries in Africa spent less than ten dollars per person on health annually and some spent as little as one dollar (Bermejo, 2004). For many Africans the price of drugs for tackling HIV remains beyond their reach.

At the Doha Trade meeting in 2001 an agreement was reached that combating health emergencies should take precedence over obligations under

TRIPS. However, the US Administration, under pressure from its own pharmaceutical lobby, continues actively to champion the rights of patent holders in bilateral trade agreements, even at the expense of poorer countries in Africa and elsewhere. The US is currently attempting to secure TRIPS-plus measures in bilateral free trade agreements with African countries, for example through the US Free Trade Agreement with the Southern African Customs Union (South Africa, Botswana and Namibia). A further agreement at the WTO in August 2003, which sought to uphold public health concerns against the demands of patent holders, is also under challenge.

There are two key flexibilities within the TRIPS agreement. Firstly, the right of poor countries to import generic versions of patented medicines, so-called 'parallel importing'. Secondly, the right of countries, where they have the capacity, to compulsorily licence the production of drugs domestically, without the approval of the patent holder. The Doha agreement and the WTO agreement of September 2003 acknowledge these flexibilities, but the capacity of African countries to use them to counter public health crises such as HIV/AIDS is under threat, particularly by US commercial interests and their allies in the US Administration.

The G8 countries should:

- Reform existing intellectual property rules to enable African and other poor countries to import generic versions of patented drugs and, where possible, to issue compulsory licences for the production of drugs; and not introduce, under any circumstances, TRIPS-plus measures into bilateral free trade agreements with African countries.

Strengthening Africa's interests in the international trading system

If African countries are to derive greater benefits from international trade, they also need a bigger and more effective voice in the international trading system. Too often the policies of the G8 countries marginalise Africa's interests in that system. There are two particular tests: firstly, the negotiations between the EU and the ACP over the proposed EPAs; secondly, the future of Special and Differential Treatment and Africa's voice within the WTO.

Economic Partnership Agreements (EPAs)

Under the Cotonou Agreement, signed in 2000, it was agreed that the European Union would negotiate EPAs with regional groups of ACP countries. These negotiations began in 2002 and they will conclude in 2007. Like the previous Lomé Agreement, Cotonou is about more than just trade; it represents a broad-based approach to partnership in development, including political cooperation, technical assistance and trade-related capacity building. In some important respects the partnership elements of Cotonou are stronger than those of Lomé. However, the issue of trade liberalisation has come increasingly to the fore in the context of EU/ACP negotiations on EPAs.

The European Commission sees EPAs as reciprocal free trade areas that it will negotiate on a bilateral basis with ACP countries or regions. This marks an important shift from the system of non-reciprocal preferences that characterised the Lomé Agreement. The change in EU policy is motivated by a combination of factors, including the need for EU/ACP trade to be compliant with current interpretations of WTO rules, the inability of ACP countries to exploit their favourable market access terms with the EU and, more controversially, by the EU's desire to get better access for its own exporters to ACP markets. Many critics of EPAs focus heavily on the last factor and argue that EPAs will be very damaging to ACP countries, particularly to infant industries in Africa that will not be able to compete with European industries (Goodison and Stoneman, 2004). The elimination of tariffs under EPAs may also reduce much-needed government revenues in Africa (ActionAid, 2004). There are, indeed, legitimate concerns about the EPA process and about its impact on Africa, particularly on the issue of reciprocity. 'Reciprocity between equals is one thing, but it hardly makes sense when one party is so much stronger than the other' (Kinnock, 2003).

African countries should be able to control the degree and pace of trade opening, in a way that is consistent with their broader development strategy. Where African countries experience transitional costs from changes in trade policies, the EU and G8 should also be prepared to provide support.

However, it is important not to diminish the role that ACP countries, including African countries, are now playing in setting out their own priorities for these negotiations. In some respects, the ACP's bargaining power and influence is more significant than ever before, and this is a development that should be welcomed.

Special and differential treatment and Africa's voice in the WTO

The concept of Special and Differential Treatment has been around for a long time in international trade policy, but its precise meaning and application remains contested. Given the disparities in wealth between Africa and the G8, it is important that the principle of special treatment should be preserved and indeed strengthened and expanded within the international trading system. That means upholding the right of African and other poorer countries to open their markets more slowly than wealthier countries, fewer administrative and procedural burdens, longer timescales for implementing agreements and more flexibility to respond to specific development issues even where this may run counter to multilateral trade rules. It should also mean increasing the 'space' for African countries to pursue trade and development strategies that may conflict with the existing trade orthodoxy (Corrales-Leal *et al.*, 2003). One of the most serious failings of the international trading system – and of the G8 countries that have largely shaped it

– has been the tendency to impose a 'one-size-fits-all' model of trade liber-alisation on all countries, including through IFI and donor conditionality (Rodrik, 2001). The circumstances of Africa and other poorer parts of the world require a more sophisticated and calibrated policy response.

These changes are more likely to occur when African and other poor countries have a bigger voice within the WTO and when the WTO's pro-cedures are reformed to facilitate Africa's effective participation. There are some encouraging developments in this regard, including the formation of the so-called 'G90', bringing together the overlapping memberships of the AU, the ACP and the LDCs, prior to the Cancun trade meeting in 2003. But more needs to be done by the G8 and others to give African countries a bigger say over the international trade agenda. Eighteen African countries still have no permanent representation at the WTO in Geneva. Enhancing Africa's capacity to negotiate trade deals that serve their interests will require increased technical and capacity building support.

G8 countries should:

- Allow ACP countries to determine the degree and pace of market open-ing, consistent with their broader development strategies, in the current negotiations with the EU on the proposed EPAs.

- Uphold the concept of Special and Differential Treatment for poor countries in Africa and elsewhere, giving these countries greater space to determine their own trade and development strategies.

- Provide practical support to African trade negotiators and ensure that trade negotiation processes provide adequate time for African countries to consult and ensure that deals are in their interests.

3 Restricting arms transfers[1]

Even in societies not beset by civil war, the easy availability of small arms has in many cases contributed to violence and political instability. These, in turn, have damaged development prospects and imperilled human security in every way.

Kofi Annan, UN Secretary General (24 September, 1999)

Despite recent and welcome moves towards peace in countries such as Angola and Burundi, significant parts of Africa continue to be affected by war and violent conflict. Over the last few decades, Africa has been the most conflict-affected region of the world. Millions of Africans have been killed, injured or displaced as a consequence of this armed conflict (DFID, 2001). Much of this violence has been deliberately targeted at civilians rather than armed groups (Klare, 2003; UN, 1998). A clear example is the devastating situation in Darfur, where civilians have been the primary victims of the violence engulfing that region of Sudan.

Violent conflict has inflicted enormous damage on Africa's development prospects and is a major cause of Africa's poverty. The impacts of conflict include the destruction of infrastructure, such as airports, electricity supplies, ports, roads and water supply, as well as social infrastructure such as schools and health clinics. Violent conflict has worsened agricultural productivity and access to food, with displaced people unable to tend their land. It has created an insecure economic environment hostile to domestic and international investment and has contributed to capital flight. And high military spending in some African countries has diverted scarce resources from more pressing development priorities. The damaging economic effects of violent conflict often outlive the conflict itself and are rarely confined to one country, with neighbouring states also suffering significant economic damage, including lower rates of economic growth (World Bank, 2003).

The causes of conflicts in Africa are complex, and a detailed analysis is beyond the remit of this chapter or report. Many of these causes are rooted in national structures and political systems, in particular: authoritarian rule, the exclusion of groups from governance, socio-economic deprivation combined with inequity, and weak states that lack the institutional capacity to manage normal political and social conflict (Nathan, 2004). Inequalities between different groups, what has been described as 'horizontal inequality', can also increase the risks of violent conflict (Stewart, 2001). Disputes over access to and control of resources can fuel conflict (see section on conflict financing in chapter 4), and there is often a strong regional dimension

[1] This report draws heavily on a joint ippr/ Saferworld submission to the UK Prime Minister's Strategy Unit in May 2004.

to conflicts, with states caught up in a series of multiple and interlocking disputes and conflicts that cross national borders.

But the world's richer countries also impact on Africa's propensity to violence, not just through the colonial or Cold War legacy, but also in the present. This chapter focuses on one specific example of this: the role of G8 governments and nationals as significant suppliers of arms and military equipment to Africa.

Arms proliferation in Africa

While the easy availability of arms does not cause Africa's violent conflicts, it usually exacerbates them, increases their destructive impact and makes them harder to resolve (Klare, 2004). It is estimated that small arms are implicated in more than 300,000 deaths each year, most of them in Africa (GIIS, 2003). Larger-scale weaponry and military equipment is also responsible for many human deaths and injuries in Africa, although accurate figures for this are not available. These deaths and injuries are the most direct and obvious human cost of arms proliferation on the continent.

Arms proliferation can also contribute to instability in African countries not involved in full-blown conflicts, making it more likely that tensions and disputes become violent. For example, the traditional practice of cattle rustling in parts of Kenya, Uganda, Ethiopia and Sudan has become much more lethal following the influx of large quantities of weapons into these countries in recent years. In Uganda, it has fuelled conflict between the heavily armed Karamoja tribe and the government (Mkutu, 2003). And the availability of weapons is fuelling violent crime in cities such as Nairobi, Lagos and Johannesburg. In South Africa, for example, firearms are used in forty-eight per cent of homicides, fifty-eight per cent of robberies, twenty-eight per cent of assaults and fourteen per cent of sexual offences (GIIS, 2004). In this sense, arms are a significant contributory cause or factor in explaining armed violence and violent conflict in Africa.

Weapons flows to Africa come from a variety of sources – both licit and illicit – and through a wide variety of means. For most of the Cold War period, the pattern of arms transfers was from the superpowers to African allies fighting in proxy wars. After 1990 the pattern changed, with central and eastern European states – countries with extensive stockpiles of military equipment – becoming the major source of weapons entering Africa. More recently, the main source of arms has shifted further to the east, with Belarus, China, Moldova and Ukraine becoming large-scale suppliers. In recent years, more than twenty-seven million dollars of small arms have been imported by African governments each year (GIIS, 2003). Armed rebel groups and private individuals or companies also import substantial quantities of weapons into Africa.

But G8 countries are also a critical part of this trade. Take the case of small arms. Of the world's seven largest exporters of small arms – the US, Italy, Belgium, Germany, Russia, Brazil and China – four are members of the G8 (GIIS, 2004).

In addition, G8 countries export heavier forms of arms and military equipment, such as tanks, aircraft and artillery to African governments (Grimmett, 2004). While some of these transfers are defensible, allowing legitimate governments to meet their legitimate security needs, other more questionable transfers have been approved. These would appear to breach undertakings made by G8 governments to enforce tight controls over weapons exports to conflict zones or to regimes or groups that abuse human rights.

Of the G8, Russia's arms export policy currently raises the biggest concerns. Russia is the largest single exporter of arms to Africa (*ibid*). Many of these arms have been transferred to rights-violating regimes and conflict zones on the continent. For example, Russia has been a major supplier of AK 47s to Zimbabwe, despite the human rights record of the Mugabe regime (Amnesty International, 2002). Russia has provided the Angolan government with attack helicopters, fighter bombers and tanks, including during the height of the conflict in 2000–1, at a time when hundreds of thousands of Angolan civilians were killed or displaced in the war against UNITA (Amnesty International, 2003). And Russia has supplied the Sudanese regime with military helicopters that have been used in attacks on rebels and civilians in west Darfur (*ibid*).

Recent developments in US arms export policy to the region are also worrying. As part of its 'war on terror', the US has approved increasing levels of military assistance to countries in North, West and East Africa, despite the State Department's reports of serious human rights abuses in some of these countries (HRW, 2005).

The UK exports relatively small amounts of military equipment to Africa (excluding South Africa), but a number of recent licensing decisions give cause for concern. An open licence (which typically allows for repeated and unlimited deliveries) was issued in 2002 for components for a wide range of offensive naval equipment for Côte d'Ivoire and Nigeria. This includes components for combat aircraft and helicopters and for machine guns, mortars and artillery. Despite continuing concerns about the human rights situation in Angola, the UK has also agreed twenty-two Single Individual Export Licences to a value of fourteen million pounds and ten Open Individual Export Licences for exports to the country. This covers the export of armoured all wheel drive vehicles, and components for machine guns, combat aircraft and combat helicopters (Foreign and Commonwealth Office, 2002).

France and Germany also export directly to the region. Questionable French deals include the supply of helicopter gunships to the government of Côte d'Ivoire following the attempted coup in September 2002 (IISS, 2004; Global Witness, 2003). German military exports to the wider region that give cause for concern include the supply of ammunition for rifles to Yemen – widely acknowledged as a supplier of small arms into Somalia.

If G8 countries are serious about reducing their contribution to violent conflict in Africa, they need to tighten significantly their controls over direct arms exports to the region. An International Arms Trade Treaty, based on states' existing responsibilities under international law, would be an important way of strengthening controls over weapons transfers. The G8 is also a particularly important forum in which to engage Russia about arms proliferation issues. And G8 countries could use their political and economic leverage to encourage more restrictive controls on the part of other key suppliers, including countries in central and eastern Europe, China and the states of the former Soviet Union. To do this effectively, G8 countries would need to pursue a combination of strategies, including diplomatic pressure but also practical support, helping countries to put in place much more effective systems for regulating arms transfers, managing arms stockpiles and destroying surplus stocks of arms.

G8 countries should:

- Establish an International Arms Trade Treaty, setting high common standards governing arms transfers to conflict-affected regions in Africa and elsewhere.

G8 arms brokers, traffickers and transport agents

Much of the weaponry available in Africa's conflict zones was transferred there by arms brokers and traffickers (intermediaries who arrange for arms to be shipped to the final destination from third countries). Today, a typical arms transfer to Africa might involve weapons sourced from the former Soviet Union, organised by a west European broker and diverted through a neighbouring country in the region.

A myriad of shady networks and transportation, finance and insurance ties often link such transfers back to G8 countries. Notorious G8 arms brokers include the Russian dealer Victor Bout. He is accused by the UN of having supplied contraband weapons to rebel movements in Angola, Sierra Leone and to the regime of Charles Taylor in Liberia. UN reports also suggest that Bout and his networks have been active in Cameroon, Central African Republic, Democratic Republic of Congo, Equatorial Guinea, Kenya, Libya, Congo-Brazzaville, Rwanda, South Africa, Sudan, Swaziland and Uganda.

Arms brokers tend to focus predominantly on small arms and light weapons. However, they also trade in heavier military equipment. According to a report by the UN Panel of Experts on the Illegal Exploitation of Natural Resources in the DRC, John Bredenkamp, a UK-based businessman, is an active investor in a brokering company called Aviation Consultancy Services, in which capacity:

> ... he has offered to mediate sales of British aerospace military equipment to the DRC. Mr Bredenkamp's representatives claimed that his companies observed EU sanctions on Zimbabwe, but British Aerospace spare parts for ZDF (Zimbabwe Defence Forces) Hawk jets were supplied in 2002 in breach of those sanctions. (UN Panel, 2002a; RAID, 2004)

One of the significant weaknesses in G8 countries' policies towards arms brokers and traffickers is the lack of adequate legal powers to curb their activities, particularly where they operate extra-territorially. The UK case is a clear example of this. The UK Government has taken steps in the Export Control Act (2002) to control the activities of arms brokers operating from within the UK. But under the new legislation, there is still nothing to stop a UK broker operating from outside the UK from transferring small arms and tanks to countries such as the Côte d'Ivoire, Rwanda or Uganda.

The UK Government has opposed the idea of extending full extra-territorial controls to the brokering of small arms, light weapons and ammunition, arguing that this would be impractical and difficult to enforce. However, the Government has not explained why it is practical to enforce extra-territorial controls on the trafficking of long-range missiles and instruments of torture but not on small arms. Nor has it explained why it is feasible to have extra-territorial controls on terrorist activity (in its Anti-Terrorism, Crime and Security Act) but not on small arms. Some countries – the US, Belgium, Estonia and Finland – already have full extra-territorial controls over arms brokers and traffickers, suggesting that the practical issues involved are not insurmountable. Another option would be for G8 governments to strengthen controls over arms brokers by establishing (and exchanging information on) white lists and black lists of arms brokers.

The means by which arms are shipped from the source country to the final destination in Africa are multiple and complex. It will often involve the manipulation of weaknesses in the regulation of international transport, as well as loopholes in national legal systems. Weapons can be transported by air, sea or across land, although air transportation is the preference of most arms dealers. In many of these cases the planes are subject to document fraud, forgery of flight plans and other irregularities, including illegal aircraft registration. One way to address this would be for G8 governments to establish black and white lists of disreputable and reputable air companies and air operators to ensure that suspect companies are not being supported by G8 governments in other circumstances, for example by being contracted to carry humanitarian relief.

False End User Certificates (EUCs) are another common means by which G8 arms brokers and traffickers arrange for arms to be illicitly transferred to Africa. An EUC is supposed to guarantee the final destination of weapons; however it can be easily forged or falsified. The UN Panel of Experts on Liberia showed that false EUCs from Nigeria were used for the delivery of over 200 tons of arms to Liberia, in violation of the arms embargo imposed on that country (UN Panel, 2002b). The role of aircraft insurance is a further critical element in the transfer of arms into Africa. There is some evidence to suggest that Russian planes and insurance companies are frequently used in this regard as they are willing to grant cheap 'no questions asked' insurance on the understanding that there will be no payouts on insurance claims. To deter individuals and companies from trafficking arms, G8 governments could ensure that legal entities registered to carry arms and military equipment insure their planes only with approved insurers.

The illicit transfer of arms to Africa is further facilitated by the complexity of corporate structures, with different systems for aircraft registration and insurance, pilot insurance, and the insurance of the cargo, the operating agent and the aircraft owner. These can all be registered in different countries. This makes it very difficult to discover the actual owners of some companies and who is responsible for specific arms deals. Many of the countries in which these companies are registered – often offshore tax havens like the British Virgin Islands – have strict privacy but weak money laundering laws. The laxity of these laws is something that G8 governments have often deliberately encouraged for commercial reasons (Palan, 2003). Effective control over the transportation of arms is also compromised by the existence of registers that allow those vessels or aircraft on their books to run their operations without adequate supervision.

A significant part of the problem of arms availability in Africa's conflict zones is caused by countries in the region with which the UK and other G8 countries have significant diplomatic and development relationships. For example, the role of Uganda and Rwanda in the DRC is well known, yet little if any pressure is being put on these countries to cease their role in arms proliferation. There is an important role for the G8 in putting pressure on such countries, as well as in providing practical support to combat arms proliferation on the continent.

G8 countries should:

- Agree common extra-territorial controls over arms brokers and push for an international agreement on arms brokering, paving the way for the establishment of an international legally-binding agreement on arms brokering at the UN Small Arms Review Conference in 2006.

- Introduce a compulsory registration scheme for arms brokers and transport agents, with failure to register leading to prosecution of the companies concerned.

- Promote international standards for the administration of shipping or aircraft registers to prevent their involvement in illegal arms transfers.

4 Curbing corruption and conflict financing

We commit to intensifying support for the adoption and implementation of effective measures to combat corruption, bribery and embezzlement.

G8 Africa Action Plan (27 June, 2002)

The international private sector has an important role to play in helping Africa to make greater progress in the reduction of poverty and the achievement of the MDGs. Well managed, inward investment flows can boost levels of economic growth, spread technology and skills, and create jobs. At present, however, investment flows to Africa, especially foreign direct investment, lag behind investments in other regions of the developing world. Africa currently accounts for less than one per cent of global capital flows. Creating a more favourable environment for inward investment, and maximising the developmental benefits of these flows, has been identified by NEPAD as a key priority, a means for 'extricating the continent from the malaise of underdevelopment and exclusion in a globalising world' (NEPAD, 2001).

G8 countries should respond by helping African countries to create a more attractive investment climate, and work with African governments and organisations such as the NEPAD Business Group to reduce real or perceived barriers to investment in Africa. This should include support for better political and corporate governance, action against crime and lawlessness, investment in infrastructure and human capital, and a reduction in the costs of establishing a business in Africa. Action in all these areas would not only help generate increased economic activity and inward investment, it should also help to counter the problem of capital flight. It is estimated that the stock of capital flight from sub-Saharan Africa is $148 billion and represents around thirty-three per cent of the private wealth of the continent. This compares with less than ten per cent in Asia or Latin America (Amoako, 2004).

But G8 countries also need to recognise that poor governance of the international private sector can severely distort and damage Africa's development prospects. These issues are particularly relevant to the extractive sector. While the emergence of Chinese and Indian companies in Africa also poses concerns in this regard, G8 companies remain the biggest players on the continent, and they are the focus of this chapter. While the best companies in the extractive sector have taken steps to address some of these issues, for example through strategies for corporate social responsibility, these have limitations (Mepham and Cooper, 2004). This chapter will look at two specific areas where stronger regulation by G8 governments is required: firstly, the contribution of G8 companies to corruption in Africa, and secondly the role of the international private sector in the financing of conflict on the continent. In both these areas, G8 countries need to clean up their act.

Tackling corruption

Corruption in Africa takes many forms: from grassroots 'petty' corruption, to the 'grand' theft of state resources by government officials. Collectively these various manifestations of corruption are fuelling conflict and human rights abuses in Africa and undermining development. In some cases, corruption has reached extreme proportions. For example, it is estimated that General Sani Abacha looted between two billion dollars and five billion dollars from Nigeria during his five-year dictatorship (Transparency International, 2004).

The direct costs of corruption obviously include the diversion of resources from more productive to less productive activities. The indirect costs include diminished incentives for domestic and inward investment (Gray and Kaufmann, 1998).

Corruption also has serious implications for political governance in Africa. Government officials may spend public resources on large projects such as defence contracts – which are more amenable to corruption – than on, say, increasing teachers' salaries (Eigen, 2002). Corruption also undermines the democratic process when agreements between authorities and businesses are bought, rather than being the result of a democratic decision-making process. Corruption creates and exacerbates inequality as, in a corrupt society, wealth reinforces power and power reinforces wealth (Gupta *et al.*, 1998). Corruption can impact negatively on citizens' rights. For example, in a system where justice is 'purchased' rather than being something that citizens can access as a right, the poor are likely to suffer most. Corruption also facilitates other forms of illicit activity, including money laundering, the drugs and arms trade, and the establishment of illegal and legal companies engaged in this trade. And it facilitates the growth of transnational crime.

Tackling corruption in Africa will clearly require more decisive action by Africans themselves. In recent years, there appears to have been a greater willingness among some African states to deal with corruption. For example, the former President of Zambia, Frederick Chiluba, is facing corruption charges in his own country (BBC, 2003). In addition, the Lesotho Prosecuting Authority has successfully prosecuted some of the world's leading construction companies for bribing officials as part of the multi-billion dollar Lesotho Highlands Water Project. African states have also started to put institutional mechanisms in place to tackle corruption more effectively. Examples include the establishment of the Economic and Financial Crimes Commission in Nigeria and the asset disclosure requirements on public officials established in both Uganda and Kenya (Goredema and Botha, 2004). At the continental level, the countries subscribing to NEPAD have pledged to clamp down on corruption – the APRM self-assessment questionnaire includes several questions directed at finding out the measures being taken to combat corruption. The AU has also launched an anti-corruption initiative in the form of the Convention on Preventing and Combating Corruption. However, so far only six countries have ratified this Convention – it needs fifteen ratifications to come into force.

But G8 countries also need to take corruption much more seriously. It takes at least two parties to engage in corrupt practices: those that give bribes as well as those that receive them. Developed country companies, including those from G8 countries, are often involved in corruption, paying large bribes to secure commercial deals.

> Big money corruption still flourishes in Africa due to deals struck in Brussels, Houston, London or Paris. These deals enrich a few Africans and their Western partners, but cheat millions of Africans out of the fruits of the continent's resources. (Amoako, 2004)

Some of these companies are even supported by cover from export credit agencies (ECAs). ECAs often underwrite contracts that include the cost of commissions a company has paid to win the contract. They have also paid out insurance to companies that have had their contracts cancelled due to allegations of corruption (Corner House, 2003). There are also concerns that companies that have been prosecuted for overseas corruption can still bid for government procurement contracts. In January 2006, a new EU Directive will come into force that disqualifies companies from bidding for EU government contracts if they have been prosecuted for corruption within the EU. However, there are two problems with this new Directive. First, there is no blacklist of companies and it relies on governments being aware of any relevant prosecutions. Second, it is unclear if a company that has been prosecuted outside the EU (for example, in Lesotho) would be rendered ineligible to bid for government contracts.

Money laundering is another key link in the chain that allows corrupt African leaders to conceal the origins of ill-gotten assets, with these resources being transferred out of the country via the international financial system. It is estimated that leaders of African countries have collectively deposited around twenty billion dollars in Swiss bank accounts alone (Corner House, 2000). Preventing the financial systems of developed countries from providing a haven for corruptly-acquired assets will require concerted international action, especially by the G8.

In recent years, the international community has taken some steps to address these issues. Perhaps the two most important initiatives regarding corruption are the OECD Convention on Combating Bribery of Foreign Public Officials in International Business Transactions and the United Nations Convention against Corruption. The international community has also put more weight behind anti-money laundering initiatives, most notably the Financial Action Task Force (FATF). G8 countries are critical to the effectiveness of these initiatives.

OECD Convention on Combating Bribery of Foreign Public Officials

The OECD Bribery Convention (1997) compels its signatories to introduce new laws that make it possible to prosecute companies in their home countries for paying bribes abroad. It also requires them to provide mutual legal assistance (when a country provides support with investigations, prosecution and judicial proceedings for another country) to facilitate inquiries into suspected violations (OECD, 1997). The Convention was signed by all thirty OECD countries and came into force in February 1999.

However, the overall impact of the OECD Convention has been weakened by limited attempts to publicise it amongst business, by loopholes in the Convention itself, by deficiencies in the OECD's monitoring process and by a serious lack of political will amongst governments. Only fifty-one per cent of the 835 business experts interviewed by the NGO Transparency International in 2002 had heard of the OECD Convention. Moreover, only thirty-five per cent had put in place compliance programmes within their companies (Transparency International, 2002). A separate OECD study in 2003 found that only forty-three of the top one hundred non-financial multinational companies presented anti-corruption material on their websites, compared with their propensity to make public statements on environmental issues (almost ninety per cent). Of these forty-three, only twenty-six mention bribery of public officials, and only seven per cent provided a formal report on implementation of their anti-corruption commitments (OECD, 2003).

The OECD Convention does not address the bribery of private officials, including officials of political parties (Transparency International, 2004). A bigger problem is that companies are not held responsible for the actions of agents or subsidiaries acting on their behalf. As a Control Risks Group Survey found in 2002, seventy per cent of US companies and over seventy-seven per cent of companies from other selected OECD countries said that they occasionally used agents to make corrupt payments for them (Control Risks Group, 2002).

There are also weaknesses with the Convention's monitoring process. Phase 1 of the process involved ensuring that each of the signatories had put in place the required national legislation. This process is carried out by Peer Review, involving representatives from two other OECD countries and from the OECD Secretariat. Phase 2 of the process, which is intended to survey the effectiveness of this legislation, has been slower than planned.

Although the process was supposed to have finished by 2005, it is now unlikely to be completed before the end of 2007.

There has also been too little enforcement by governments of their anti-bribery commitments. For example, not a single UK national has so far been prosecuted. While some OECD countries have successfully prosecuted a company under these new laws, of the G8 only the US and France have prosecuted their nationals for foreign bribery offences – and these have been relatively small in scale (OECD, 2004). One of the reasons for this is that it is complex and potentially expensive to prove bribery, particularly when the alleged abuse takes place in Africa. The weakness of legal and governance structures in many African countries is a serious obstacle to obtaining the necessary evidence to bring a successful prosecution.

But a large part of the explanation also lies with the low priority that G8 countries have given to the issue and, in particular, to bringing prosecutions. This is a particular issue in the UK. The Phase 2 monitoring review of the UK's compliance with the OECD Convention is currently underway and will be made publicly available in March 2005. It is widely anticipated that this will be critical of the UK Government, highlighting a lack of serious investigations of alleged cases of corruption overseas and a failure to bring any actual prosecutions. Since June 2004, the Serious Fraud Office (SFO) has taken the lead role in dealing with this issue. While this is a welcome development, there are still serious concerns that not enough police resources are available to the SFO for it to pursue investigations successfully.

United Nations Convention against Corruption

The most recent and comprehensive attempt to address corruption has been led by the United Nations. In December 2003, ninety-five countries signed the UN Convention against Corruption. This must be ratified by at least thirty-five states before it can come into force. To date, only thirteen countries have ratified it (United Nations Office of Drugs and Crime). No G8 country has yet done so and there is a real danger that thirty smaller countries will be the first to ratify, thereby bringing it into force without the weight of G8 countries behind it.

The Convention includes developing as well as developed countries. It also goes further than the OECD Convention, with more rigorous provisions on the return of assets stolen by corrupt leaders to their country of origin, anti-money laundering measures and provisions for enhanced mutual legal assistance and international cooperation (Bray, 2003).

However, the Convention also falls short in a number of important areas. It is a mixture of mandatory and voluntary directives. For example, the articles on the criminalisation of illicit enrichment and bribery are not binding. In addition, corruption in the political sector is only subject to a non-mandatory framework. Payments to political parties are also not covered in the Convention, a result of strong US pressure (*ibid*).

CENTRAL BOOKS

99 Wallis Road, London E9 5LN
Tel: UK 0845 458 9911 International + 44 20 85
Fax: UK 0845 458 9912 International + 44 20 85
Email: orders@centralbooks.com
VAT registration Number GB 232 2069 02

Magazine Department 44(0) 845 458 992
Email: magazines@centralbooks.com

Delivery Address:

Graham Leicester
3 East Grange
St Andrews
Fife
KY16 8LL

Accounts Office:
Graham Leicester
3 East Grange
St Andrews
Fife
KY16 8LL

ISBN	Customer Reference	Quantity	Description
1860302661	IPPR SUB	1	Putting Our House in Order

5 8800
25 8879

Invoice SS

Invoice Number	Date (Tax Point)	Date for Payment
I534721	24/02/2005	31/03/2005

Account Number	VAT Number
39010L	

	Format	Pub. Price £ or Report	Discount Rate %	Trade Price £	VAT Rate %	Trade Value £
	PBK	9.95	Free			

Sub Total	Post & Packing	Total VAT	Total
0.00	0.00	0.00	**0.00**

Items: 1
Weight: 0.20Kg

As with all initiatives, the success of the UN Convention will depend on how well it is implemented. The absence of a mechanism to monitor compliance is worrying. The monitoring process will only be decided at the Conference of State Parties that is convened one year after the Convention comes into force. States are also able to ratify the Convention with reservations. If this opportunity is used by many states, there is a danger that the UN Convention will be significantly weakened.

Financial Action Task Force

In response to mounting concern over money laundering, a group of OECD countries established the FATF on money laundering in 1989. The FATF, which currently has thirty-one country members, has adopted a set of 'forty recommendations' – measures national governments should take to implement effective anti-money laundering programmes. The FATF was initially set up to respond to the issue of drug trafficking and organised crime; more recently funding for terrorism has been added to its concerns. The FATF has not, however, focused on laundering of money stolen from poor country taxpayers nor on the profits of trade from poor country conflict zones.

Moreover, the implementation of the FATF's recommendations is effectively being left up to FATF-style regional bodies. The Eastern and Southern Africa Anti-Money Laundering Group (ESAAMLG) is the only regional body within Africa. This body does not include large countries with a history of corruption such as Nigeria and Angola. A key role for G8 countries should be to support the ESAAMLG, which is under-resourced and lacks capacity to undertake evaluations, as well as to support the development of a West African Anti-Money Laundering Group.

The FATF has drawn up a list of 'non-cooperative countries and territories' that it says falls short of FATF criteria. It uses these effective blacklists to try and influence governments and elites within these states to address money laundering issues more robustly. There has been some evidence to suggest that these blacklists do indeed influence behaviour of non-compliant states (Levi, 2002). However, the effectiveness of the blacklist is being hampered by a current freeze on adding new countries to the list. There are also concerns that the FATF does not apply the same principles to more powerful nations such as the US, which in 2001 was in full compliance with only seventeen of the twenty-eight Task Force recommendations requiring specific country action (IMF, 2001).

G8 countries should:

- Close loopholes in the OECD Convention on Combating Bribery of Foreign Public Officials and provide additional resources to investigate and prosecute G8 companies that engage in corruption abroad.

- Ratify the UN Convention against Corruption.

- Deny export credit guarantees, government procurement and other forms of government support, for a specified period, to companies found to have engaged in corrupt practices abroad.

- Provide additional resources to provide sufficient mutual legal assistance to African countries investigating international corruption charges.

- Revitalise the FATF blacklist to allow more non-cooperative countries to be placed on it and increase the provision of technical assistance and financing for FATF-style regional bodies in Africa.

Restricting conflict financing

Over recent years, the relationship between international private sector activity and state weakness, failure and conflict has become a major research theme, as well as a growing priority for governments and international institutions. A particular focus of attention has been the apparent connection between conflict and dependence on natural resources. Intra-state conflicts in countries such as Angola, Liberia, Sierra Leone and the DRC suggested an important linkage. Commentators and politicians also seized on the theme, talking of 'diamond wars' and 'resource conflicts'.

The World Bank's research on this issue is striking and in some quarters controversial. It indicates that African and other poor countries face substantially higher risks of violent conflict, instability and poor governance if they are highly dependent on natural resources (Bannon and Collier, 2003). The Bank's work on this issue has often been characterised as explaining conflict by reference to 'greed' rather than 'grievance'.

While the Bank's work has been criticised – not least for downplaying the significance of grievances in explaining conflict and social instability – few now dispute that economic factors matter to conflict dynamics, or that better management of natural resources can help to reduce some of the risks of conflict and instability (Ballentine and Sherman, 2003; Banfield *et al.*, 2003).

In many African countries today, violent conflict and the arms purchases that fuel them are closely linked to the exploitation of natural resources. The purchase of arms and military equipment is expensive. While many African governments have established defence sectors and funding sources that support them, others are reliant on less formal (sometimes illicit) forms of income generation to support their arms purchases. African armed groups in opposition to a government also need to find a regular source of income to assemble, equip and maintain a fighting force.

Before the end of the Cold War, many African governments and rebel groups received financial and military support from one of the superpowers or from regional powers. With the end of the Cold War, this type of aid has largely dried up. In some cases, such as Mozambique, the withdrawal of external support helped encourage former combatant parties to enter peace agreements. In others, however, it has merely encouraged combatant forces to seek out alternative forms of financing for their arms purchases and military campaigns.

African governments and rebel groups can raise funds through the direct sale or looting of resources, such as oil, diamonds, coltan and timber. In Liberia, for example, the government used natural resource exploitation and other means to fund both illegal arms purchases and illegal supplies of arms to rebels in Sierra Leone. Governments can also exploit the resources of neighbouring states to raise funds, including for military purchases. Angola, Namibia, Rwanda, Uganda and Zimbabwe all intervened in the conflict in the DRC in part to gain access to resources there (Ganesan and Vines, 2004).

This linkage between natural resources and violent conflict has very important implications for G8 countries, whose companies and consumers are heavily involved in the extraction and consumption of these resources from Africa. A variety of international initiatives has been developed over recent years to address different aspects of this problem. Most have had fairly limited impact. This section now considers briefly some of the more important of these initiatives, and suggests how G8 countries can and should strengthen them.

The OECD Guidelines on Multinational Enterprises

The longest-standing initiative for promoting high corporate standards is the OECD Guidelines on Multinational Enterprises. First adopted in 1976, these set out a comprehensive list of guidelines for good corporate behaviour, including on human rights. The latest revision of the Guidelines began in November 1998 and concluded with the adoption of a revised text by the OECD Ministerial Meeting in June 2000. While the Guidelines do not deal directly with the issue of conflict, they have been used in recent years to draw attention to the responsibilities of international companies that operate in conflict countries in Africa and elsewhere.

For example, in October 2002, the UN Expert Panel on the Illegal Exploitation of the Natural Resources of the Democratic Republic of the Congo named more than fifty OECD companies as being in breach of the OECD Guidelines in its report to the UN Security Council (UN Panel, 2002). The UN Panel sent information on some of these companies to the National Contact Points (NCPs) in the various OECD countries. However, as yet, only very limited evaluations of the Panel's accusations have been or are being conducted by NCPs in Belgium, Canada, Finland, France, the Netherlands, the UK and the US. NCPs, including in the UK, have argued that the information provided by the UN was patchy and incomplete and provided insufficient grounds on which to take action. While there is truth in these criticisms of the UN report, it is also the case that the NCPs have, in general, shown limited commitment to investigate the allegations themselves.

The Extractive Industries Transparency Initiative

Another important recent development is the Extractive Industries Transparency Initiative (EITI), launched in September 2002 and co-ordinated by the UK Department for International Development. It is now a multi-stakeholder partnership of oil and mining companies, northern and developing country governments and NGOs. It was established partly as a response to an international NGO campaign 'Publish What You Pay', which called for greater transparency over the revenue payments made to host developing country governments by international oil, mining and gas companies. The campaign has demonstrated that a lack of transparency damages human rights and development and is a source of corruption, conflict and instability, particularly in some African countries.

In Africa, Nigeria and Ghana are the only two countries currently implementing the EITI. However, a number of other countries have committed to sign up to the principles, including those of the Franc Zone (eg DRC, Gabon and Cameroon). The challenge to the EITI is twofold: to increase the number of countries implementing it, and to enhance its effectiveness. In order for the initiative to be extended to more countries, additional resources will need to be made available. Another key concern about the EITI is that it is purely voluntary. While the best G8 companies are engaging with it, there is no guarantee that all companies will do so, particularly in those countries that need it most. Making the requirement for revenue transparency 'mandatory' would significantly strengthen the initiative's impact. G8 countries should also provide increased resources to African civil society to interpret and use the newly available data.

The IFIs – whose policies are very largely determined by G8 countries – also have an important role in relation to EITI. For example, the IMF has played a constructive role in respect of Liberia and Angola in pressing for greater budgetary transparency, and the World Bank is beginning to take this issue more seriously, although it needs to do more (World Bank Operations Evaluation Department, 2003). IFIs also have an important role to play in developing international best practice, including through the development of a model template for natural resource management.

The Kimberley Process

The Kimberley Process Certification Scheme is a specific initiative designed to stop the flow of 'conflict diamonds' onto the world market. It was launched in January 2003 following widespread concern about the trade in diamonds in exacerbating conflict and large-scale human rights abuses in countries such as Angola and Sierra Leone. The certification process requires governments and the diamond industry to implement import/export control regimes in the rough diamond trade, to prevent them fuelling war and human rights abuses.

However, trade in conflict diamonds still exists and there is considerable scope for strengthening the process. At present, the Kimberley Process is a system of self-regulation, which aims to track diamonds from the point of mining to the point of sale. To date, little has been done by the diamond industry to monitor and assess how self-regulation is working in practice (Global Witness, 2004). In a number of surveys amongst retailers in the UK, US, Belgium, Australia, France, Germany, Italy and Switzerland, Amnesty International and Global Witness demonstrated that many companies failed to provide adequate details about their systems of warranties and meaningful guarantees that diamonds were conflict free (Amnesty International and Global Witness, 2004).

In October 2003, the European Commission, South Africa and other governments adopted a voluntary peer review mechanism. This represents a step towards better monitoring. However, the effectiveness of such a system will depend on all countries being reviewed thoroughly at least every four years. There are currently no sanctions for those members found to be in violation of the scheme.

EU Action Plan on Forest Law Enforcement, Governance and Trade

The role of the timber trade in fuelling conflicts in Africa has only recently been acknowledged and action has so far been limited. The UN Security Council and Global Witness have published several reports that have highlighted how timber has contributed to armed conflict in the Mano River Region of Africa (Liberia, Sierra Leone and Guinea). In the case of Liberia, President Charles Taylor used the country's logging industry as a platform to prolong regional violence and traffic arms, and for personal enrichment (UN Security Council, 2000; Global Witness, 2002).

In response to this, African governments and donor agencies came together at the Africa Law Enforcement and Governance (AFLEG) Conference in October 2003. The conference examined ways in which partnerships between producers and consumers, donors, civil society and the private sector could potentially address illegal forest exploitation and associated trade in Africa, and resulted in the endorsement of a Ministerial Declaration and Action Plan for AFLEG. However, the Declaration focused heavily on voluntary actions. Many stakeholders regard these measures as insufficient to deal with the magnitude of the problem (Royal Institute for International Affairs, 2003)

In May 2003, the EU drew up an Action Plan on Forest Law Enforcement, Governance and Trade (FLEGT) (European Commission, 2003). This initiative aims to tackle the trade in illegal logging through voluntary licensing schemes and the development of voluntary partnership agreements. At present, there is no legislation in the EU prohibiting the import of illegally sourced timber (FERN *et al.*, 2004).

Alongside these specific initiatives, there would be real advantages in introducing a clearer overarching international framework of corporate accountability. The most serious attempt at this is the Norms on the Responsibilities of Transnational Corporations and other Business Enterprises with regard to Human Rights (known as the Norms), adopted unanimously by the UN Sub-commission on the Promotion and Protection of Human Rights in August 2003.

Despite attacks from important industry groups such as the International Chamber of Commerce and the Confederation of British Industry, as well as the US Government, in April 2004 the Commission on Human Rights adopted a resolution that clarified the obligations and responsibilities of businesses with regard to human rights. The UN High Commissioner for Human Rights is due to submit a report in March 2005 in response to the Norms.

The Norms are an attempt to rationalise the existing standards relating to companies' human rights responsibilities. This is particularly important as many current initiatives apply only to specific industries and do not have widespread applicability. The Norms are based on existing international human rights law and apply to all 'transnational corporations and other businesses'. As a consequence, they will help to level the playing field between companies and open them up to competitive comparison.

It is critical that the Norms are kept on the political agenda. One mechanism for this would be the appointment of a special advisor to the UN High Commissioner for Human Rights. The special advisor would report back to the Commission on Human Rights on the scope and applicability of international standards to companies and the responsibilities of states to hold their companies to account. If appointed by the UN Secretary-General, this position could carry real weight and keep the UN Norms on the agenda.

G8 countries should:

- Provide increased support to the OECD Guidelines on Multinational Enterprises and the role of the NCP system in individual countries, strengthening its capacity to investigate allegations of corporate malpractice.

- Strengthen the EITI, by introducing an industry-wide mandatory requirement on companies to disclose net revenues to all national governments, and provide support for civil society in African countries to interpret and use the newly available data.

- Press the International Financial Institutions to develop a model template for the governance of natural resource revenues and to promote revenue transparency by governments and companies in all the resource-rich African countries they work with.

- Strengthen the Kimberley Process on conflict diamonds, by supporting the establishment of a regular independent monitoring mechanism.

- Promote the EU Action Plan on FLEGT, by legislating against the import of illegal timber into the EU to allow law enforcement agencies to investigate and prosecute companies and individuals that do so.

- Support the UN Norms on the Responsibilities of Business through the appointment of a special advisor to the UN High Commissioner for Human Rights.

5 Addressing climate change[2]

For our countries, climate change is more catastrophic than terrorism.

Tanzanian delegate to the 10th Conference of Parties of the UN
Framework Convention on Climate Change (6 December, 2004)

The UN's Intergovernmental Panel on Climate Change (IPCC) concludes that there is no longer any reasonable doubt that human-induced emissions of greenhouse gases, particularly carbon dioxide released in the combustion of fossil fuels (such as coal, oil and gas), are largely to blame for global warming and climate change (IPCC, 2001a). Average global surface temperature has already risen by about 0.8°C since 1860. The IPCC forecasts a further 1.4°C to 5.8°C rise by 2100, depending on the scale of fossil fuel burning and the sensitivity of the global climate system to the accumulation of greenhouse gases. On land, the average temperature increases are likely to be greater.

However, the major producers of greenhouse gas emissions are not those who will suffer the most from their consequences. G8 countries account for around fifty per cent of these global greenhouse gas emissions, with the US the worst offender, and yet in the future climate variability will disproportionately impact upon Africa and other poorer parts of the world (Blair, 2004). Africa's climate is set to become hotter and much more variable, with increases in the frequency and intensity of severe weather. This will be enormously damaging to the prospects for development, better governance and more capable states in Africa.

Climate change will greatly exacerbate Africa's current variable and unpredictable climate. Climate extremes on the continent, such as droughts, floods and cyclones, have had significant adverse economic impacts over recent years. Large amounts of emergency aid have been allocated to respond to them, directing resources away from longer-term development.

The problem is compounded by the fact that currently Africa's population is highly vulnerable to changes in climate and has a low capacity to adapt to them. This high vulnerability is a result of the persistence of extreme poverty, the impacts of frequent natural disasters and a structure of agricultural production that is heavily dependent upon rainfall (Huq *et al.*, 2003). It is further reinforced by weak and fragile governance structures in many African countries and the impact of HIV/AIDS. Meanwhile, African countries' capacity to adapt is low, due to a lack of economic and technological resources.

G8 countries therefore have a clear obligation to act now to assist African countries in adapting to climate change, while also preventing

2 The ippr, in conjunction with the Center for American Progress in Washington DC and the Australia Institute in Canberra, established a high-level International Taskforce on Climate Change in 2004. This chapter draws on some of the research conducted for the Taskforce, whose interim conclusions were published in January 2005.

further climate change by significantly reducing their emissions of greenhouse gases.

The likely impacts of climate change on Africa

The African continent is warmer today than it was 100 years ago, with the warmest five years of the last century having occurred since 1988 (IPCC, 2001b). Africa has also experienced extreme weather events in recent years, such as the floods in Mozambique in the winter of 1999–2000, which made 1.2 million people homeless. While scientists are not yet able to conclude that such events are the direct result of climate change, they do state that they are representative of the sorts of impacts that can be expected to occur with increasing frequency as climate change accelerates.

The IPCC concludes that rising temperatures, increased extreme weather events and sea level rise will have a major impact on Africa during the course of this century. These changes will have adverse effects on food security, water availability, human health, infrastructure, natural resources, and patterns of human displacement and migration (*ibid*).

More than half of the African population is rural and directly dependent on locally grown crops or food harvested from the immediate environment. Yet over the last thirty years food production in most of Africa has not kept pace with population increases. Africa's food security situation is likely to worsen significantly as a consequence of climate change. This will result in rising temperatures and changing patterns of rainfall, causing droughts, an extension in the range of crop pests, and an increase in the frequency and intensity of extreme weather events, including heat waves, tropical storms and floods. The IPCC concludes that these changes will decrease grain yields and diminish food security, particularly in smaller African food-importing countries (*ibid*).

Climate change is expected to exacerbate desertification. Desertification in Africa has already reduced the potential productivity of one quarter of the continent's land area, significantly reducing the ability of the land to support people living on it (*ibid*). This problem will worsen as climate change leads to reductions in average annual rainfall and soil moisture in large areas of the continent, especially in southern, North and West Africa (*ibid*). This will lower the production of staple foodstuffs, such as rice, wheat and potatoes (Huq *et al.*, 2003).

Climate change is projected to reduce access to fresh water for many Africans. By 2025, an estimated 600 million Africans could be living in water-stressed environments (IPCC, 2001b). Mediterranean and southern countries in Africa are projected to be particularly badly affected. This anticipated decline in water availability and food security will increase the incidence of dehydration, malnutrition and hunger and the need for emergency food aid (*ibid*).

Climate change is also projected to extend the range of vectors of infectious disease, particularly that of malaria-carrying mosquitoes (*ibid*). Waterborne diseases, such as cholera and dysentery, are expected to affect greater numbers of Africans as a result of increased flooding following higher levels of rainfall (Huq *et al.*, 2003). The capacity of many African countries to adapt to the health problems that will result from climate change will be undermined by the HIV/AIDS pandemic, which has significantly weakened health infrastructure within Africa.

The threat to infrastructure from increases in flooding due to very heavy rainfall and increases in other extreme weather events such as tropical storms, will be compounded by sea level rise resulting from climate change. The IPCC concludes that coastal settlements in the Gulf of Guinea, Senegal, Egypt and along the east-southern African coast will be affected adversely by sea level rise (IPCC, 2001b). More than one quarter of Africa's population live within a hundred kilometres of the coast and projections suggest that the numbers at risk from coastal flooding will rise from one million in 1990 to seventy million in 2080 (DFID, 2004a). The resulting human displacement – and the health, capacity and resource issues it presents – will impact significantly on development and threaten already fragile government systems.

Another problem facing African countries is the impact that climate change is projected to have on natural resources, on which a number of African countries are heavily dependent. For example, forests cover one sixth of Africa's land area and climate change is projected to impact negatively on populations dependent on forest species for subsistence needs, as well as on that part of the economy based on forest products. In addition, the projected extinction of significant varieties of African plant and animal species is likely to impact on rural livelihoods, tourism and genetic resources (IPCC, 2001b).

The responsibilities of G8 countries

Strengthening Africa's capacity to adapt to climate change
Some degree of climate change is now inevitable, even if all greenhouse gas emissions were stopped immediately, and Africa is likely to suffer disproportionately from its impacts. It is therefore essential that G8 countries, which are most responsible for the problem, accept greater responsibility for assisting African countries to adapt to climate change. This will require a step change in the level of funding and technical support provided for adaptation policies and capacity building.

To date, the Global Environment Facility – the funding arm of all the multilateral environmental agreements, including the United Nations Framework Convention on Climate Change (UNFCCC) – has allocated less than ten per cent of its climate change spending to adaptation (Huq, 2005).

In 2001 a number of new funds were created, including the Adaptation Fund and the Special Climate Change Fund, but they have yet to disburse resources. In addition, the EU and other G8 countries made a 'political declaration' at the 7th Conference of the Parties of the UNFCCC in 2001 to provide $450 million a year for adaptation. Three years on, however, only $20 million has been provided (*ibid*).

As a first step, G8 countries should honour their existing commitments. Beyond that, each G8 government should commit to providing much greater and more predictable revenue streams: an essential requirement for building the adaptive capacity of the poorest and most vulnerable countries. Some of this funding could be obtained by diverting the subsidies granted by developed countries to their own polluting fossil fuel industries – conservatively estimated at around seventy-three billion dollars per year during the late 1990s (nef, 2004).

G8 countries should provide resources to the already-established 'Marrakech Funds' for adaptation. For the long term, a new mechanism should be created to guarantee revenues for adaptation more effectively. This should involve contributions being linked, in part at least, to countries' responsibilities for climate impacts, putting into effect the 'polluter pays' principle enshrined in the UNFCCC (Huq, 2005). By the end of 2005, there will be a scientific methodology for calculating emissions contributions, which will enable this to happen. This is a result of work by the 'Ad-hoc group for the modelling and assessment of contributions to climate change' (MATCH). This could be used to help determine equitable financial contributions.

Enabling African countries to adapt to climate change will also require G8 countries and the IFIs to mainstream adaptation issues into their development assistance strategies for Africa. All too often, as a World Bank report concluded, 'climate risks are not well assessed in project preparation and in Country Assistance Strategies' (Burton and van Aalst, 1999). A significant amount of G8 development aid is invested in infrastructure such as roads and bridges, which have relatively long life spans. Funding agencies should be required to take climate change into account in the design and construction stages of these projects, to ensure that infrastructure investment is 'climate proofed'.

Climate change also needs to be factored into development policy relating to water, agriculture, PRSs and coastal zone management. Policy-makers should apply vulnerability or impact assessments to all new policies, to exclude actions that might put vulnerable communities at greater risk. Doing so is well worth the investment. It has been estimated that a rise in sea level of half a metre would cause about $250 million worth of losses along the Eritrean coastal zone; the construction of sea defences would cost only fifty million dollars (Huq *et al.*, 2003).

But acting preventatively will require better systems for monitoring and assessment. According to DFID, 'The African climate observation system is in a worse state than that on any continent and is deteriorating' (DFID, 2004b). The G8 should put substantial, long-term funding into programmes that build the climate observation and prediction capacity of African societies, thereby providing firmer foundations for future adaptive policies. G8 countries should also require their own climate research institutes to look at expected climate impacts for different regions in Africa and to consider best practice policies, technologies and livelihood strategies to cope with expected climatic risks. And G8 countries should commit to help build the capacity of African policy-makers to carry out appropriate reforms domestically and to take part in international negotiations on adaptation (Huq, 2005).

Reducing global emissions
While it may be possible for African countries to adapt to some climatic impacts if adequate assistance is provided, it will be impossible to do so if climate change is allowed to continue unabated.

Action by most G8 countries to curb their CO_2 emissions has fallen far short of what is necessary. The United States is responsible for twenty-five per cent of global emissions, although it constitutes only 4.6 per cent of the world's population (nef, 2003). To date, the US has refused to ratify the Kyoto Protocol and figures suggest that the current Bush energy plan would actually leave US emissions twenty-five per cent higher in 2010 than in 1990, compared with the seven per cent cut that the US agreed to when originally negotiating in Kyoto (*ibid*). US officials have also sought to delay action further by announcing another five years of technical investigations, aimed at developing scientific forecasts, before deciding how best to address the problem.

While all the other members of the G8 have now ratified the Kyoto Protocol, which entered into legal force in February 2005, several are set to miss their Kyoto targets on current trends, including Italy, Germany (European Environment Agency, 2004), Japan (Hall, 2004) and Canada, unless policies change.

While the UK Government will meet its Kyoto target, it is set to fall significantly short of meeting its voluntary target to reduce CO_2 emissions by twenty per cent by 2010 from 1990. The Government's own projections suggest a five per cent shortfall. UK efforts have also been undermined by the watering down of the targets set for UK industry under the first phase of the EU emissions trading scheme – which allows companies that beat their targets to sell their excess carbon credits to industries that miss their targets (Mitchell and Woodman, 2004).

It is essential that all G8 and other industrialised countries meet their domestic and Kyoto commitments to reduce their greenhouse gas emissions. This will require strong political leadership, particularly from European countries, to ensure that commitments to long-term climate security take precedence over short-term economic interests. It is equally essential that those G8 and other industrialised countries that have not yet ratified Kyoto adopt mandatory targets to reduce their greenhouse emissions as a matter of urgency.

However, this would only be a first step. Even if all the original Kyoto targets were met in full, this would only reduce CO_2 emissions from industrialised countries by five per cent below 1990 levels by 2008–12. That is certainly insufficient. To prevent serious climatic impacts, scientific evidence suggests global average temperature will need to be prevented from rising more than 2°C above the pre-industrial level (Retallack, 2005). Global average temperature has already risen by 0.8°C since 1860 and the IPCC predicts that there will be a further rise of between 1.4°C and 5.8°C by 2100, depending on the scale of fossil fuel burning (IPCC, 2001a).

To have a high chance of limiting temperature rise to 2°C, global CO_2 emission reductions of ten per cent below 1990 levels will need to be achieved by 2020 and, over the longer term, global emission reductions of about sixty per cent will be needed by 2050 and about ninety per cent by 2100 (Retallack, 2005).

Progress towards achieving such cuts should be made in the negotiations at the UN that are due to start in 2005. These are focused on what should follow the first stage of the Kyoto Protocol. In the negotiations, it is critical that G8 and other industrialised countries pledge to take on deeper emission reductions. It is also important that ways are found to engage African and other developing countries more effectively, without which climate change will not be addressed adequately. Many African governments are deeply sceptical of efforts to impose constraints or limits on their emissions. Overcoming that scepticism will require G8 and other industrialised countries to accept that any framework for future climate commitments should be based on the principles of equity and common but differentiated responsibility.

While a contraction in global emissions is clearly necessary, there also needs to be a convergence between countries in respect of their future entitlements to emit CO_2. That means recognising that a country's share of global emissions should eventually reflect its share of the world's population (Meyer, 2000). An immediate per capita allocation of all international emissions would be difficult to implement, but it could be achieved over time, with the help of emissions trading mechanisms provided for under the Kyoto Protocol.

Applying such a framework internationally would require industrialised countries to cut their emissions significantly, while many developing countries could increase theirs, at least in the short to medium term. There would need to be a period of adjustment – probably lasting several decades – in which nations' quotas converge on the same per capita level (Juniper, 2003). Many African and other poor countries would be allocated larger emissions entitlements than they currently need. Under a global emissions trading system they could then sell these emissions rights, generating resources that could be used to tackle poverty and promote sustainable development (*ibid*).

Promoting renewable sources of energy in Africa

As African and other developing countries build energy infrastructures to meet the needs of their citizens, millions of whom are currently without electricity, it is critical that G8 and other industrialised countries do more to help ensure that these new energy infrastructures do not exacerbate climate change.

This means that G8 countries should support the deployment of technologies based on harnessing renewable sources of energy. Renewable energy technologies are crucial not only to reduce greenhouse gas emissions, but also to limit both developed and developing countries' dependence on fossil fuels. With the prospect of any substantial increase in world oil production uncertain, and with the security situation in many oil-producing countries (including in West Africa) deteriorating, there is a clear and urgent need to develop alternative sources of energy. The development of low-carbon economies would also remove some of the problems that dependence on fossil fuels creates for oil-rich African countries: changing the way in which G8 and other industrialised countries interact with them, and removing a source of violent conflict on the continent (see conflict financing in chapter 4).

Renewables also make sense for African countries with large rural populations without access to electricity. In the developing world, solar is already the low-cost alternative for remote, off-grid locations that require power. Several countries have established their own photovoltaic (PV) manufacturing industries, including Kenya, which has the highest per capita PV penetration rate in the world, with 100,000 systems sold and 20,000 added annually. South Africa has plans to install 350,000 solar home systems and provide solar electricity to rural schools and clinics (Dunn, 2000).

However, much more could be done. According to the G8 Renewables Task Force, the barriers to the deployment of renewable energy are largely political and financial, rather than technological (G8 Renewables Task Force, 2001). At present, there is too little human and institutional capacity to support renewable energy projects and markets, there are high upfront costs, and there are weak incentives and policies for expanding renewable energy sources (Hampton, 2005). Greater commitment and political will by G8 countries could help to change some of these incentive structures. Key to that process is levelling the playing field between fossil fuels and renewables. Fossil fuels currently account for about four-fifths of the global primary energy supply, with oil satisfying over forty per cent of energy consumption. But this is mainly a consequence of the large subsidies and other financial incentives given to fossil fuels worldwide, and the failure properly to internalise the cost of the environmental and social damage they cause. Global subsidies for energy between 1995 and 1998 amounted to $244 billion globally, of which only nine billion dollars was for renewables (*ibid*).

A similar pattern of financial support is evident in the IFIs. In 2003, fossil fuel projects represented eighty-six per cent of the World Bank's lending in the energy sector, with just fourteen per cent for renewable energy (Simms *et al.*, 2004). The World Bank's Extractive Industries Review called on the World Bank Group to increase aggressively investments in renewable energies, by twenty per cent annually (World Bank, 2004). This renewables target was accepted in principle. However, the twenty per cent increase will be measured from 2005, in which renewables support pledged by the Bank will amount to $200 million, whereas support in some years has been as much as twice this total. G8 and other governments should ask the World Bank to review its policy and increase its renewables target.

G8 countries should also do more to overcome the view of renewables as 'second class' technologies and support initiatives such as the Renewable Energy and Energy Efficiency Partnership (REEEP). Backed by governments and financial and business professionals, and working through regional offices, REEEP facilitates financing for clean energy projects, helps underwrite the risks of project implementation, shares best practice on policy and regulation, and raises awareness.

G8 countries should:

- Implement the 'polluter pays principle' to achieve appropriate burden sharing for adaptation financing.

- Commit to global emission reductions of ten per cent below 1990 levels by 2020, and build international support for action that will keep temperature increases to no more than 2°C above pre-industrial levels.

- Work towards an equitable system of emissions entitlements, based on a per capita allowance.

- Reduce domestic and international fossil fuel subsidies, and introduce greater commercial incentives for renewable energy technologies.

- Provide increased funding for African countries to adapt to current levels of climate change, and ensure that adaptation issues are mainstreamed into all forms of development assistance towards Africa.

Conclusion – holding G8 countries to account

This report has demonstrated that in some important respects G8 countries' existing policies are damaging and disadvantaging Africa. Poor quality aid and inappropriate conditionality, unfair international trade rules, arms transfers, poor regulation of G8 companies that invest in Africa and trade in conflict commodities, and high greenhouse gas emissions – these are all areas in which current G8 policy is hindering rather than helping African reformers to make greater progress in development on their continent.

The report has argued that G8 countries need to 'put their own house in order' on these issues. Greater political will on the part of G8 governments is critical to secure the necessary changes in policy. But this is much more likely to occur if there is sustained and vigorous public pressure on G8 governments to act differently, and if G8 governments are held properly and publicly to account for the impact of their policies on Africa. Increasingly, African countries are being urged to be more accountable and to subject their policy performance to external evaluation, for example through the NEPAD Peer Review Mechanism and the UNECA Governance Report. But there is no truly comparable process for G8 countries. As the former Director General of the World Bank's Operations Evaluation Department has put it:

> No integrated effort is underway to evaluate the development effectiveness of rich countries' policies. They have escaped systematic scrutiny even though they determine the amount and quality of aid, debt reduction, foreign investment, trade, migration, access to intellectual property and global environmental trends on which sustainable development depends. (Picciotto, 2004)

In recent years there have been a number of proposals to address what is often described as 'policy incoherence' towards Africa and other poorer parts of the world on the part of wealthier countries such as the G8. The key concern has been that developed countries should not take away with one hand what they give with the other, and that they should ensure that their broader economic and foreign policies – in areas such as trade, investment or arms exports – are consistent with their stated objectives for international development (IDC, 2004).

Of course, policy coherence for development is not something that is easy to implement. All governments are trying to satisfy different constituencies and fulfil multiple objectives at any one time, and these constituencies and objectives will often conflict. However, better decision-making processes of can make these choices and tensions more transparent. In many cases, the barriers to better policy are vested interests and there are potential win-win solutions if these interests can be overcome. For example, both Africans and G8 consumers would benefit from phasing out agricultural subsidies. In other cases, there may be some short-term costs associated with the promotion of better G8 policy towards Africa. However, the 'structural adjustment' required of G8 countries in these circumstances would be significantly less than that routinely required of African countries as part of policy conditionality imposed by donors. What is important is that these choices and costs of G8 policy incoherence towards Africa should be openly acknowledged, debated and addressed.

To a limited extent this is beginning to happen. Most international communiqués and reports now include some reference to the need for policy coherence. For example, it is an important part of the eighth MDG (MDG 8 – Building a global partnership for development) and it features in the Monterrey Consensus on Financing for Development that emerged from the UN Financing for Development Conference in 2002 and the Communiqué of the World Summit for Sustainable Development in 2002. Other initiatives – including the Strategic Partnership with Africa, the Africa Partnership Forum and the G8 Africa Action Plan – have sought to develop a more comprehensive policy approach towards Africa.

But progress in implementing these commitments has been very disappointing. Genuinely independent reporting, increased capacity and resources, better analysis and a refined methodology for assessing coherence issues – these can all help in holding G8 and other developed countries to account for the combined impact of their policies on Africa.

A particularly interesting and important recent initiative on coherence is that taken by the Development Assistance Committee (DAC) of the OECD and UNECA. They are developing the idea of 'mutual accountability', where both Africans and their development partners in OECD countries are held to account for their commitments and actions (Amoako, 2004). The first full report is due to be published in 2005, and subsequent reports will be produced biennially. On the African side, this initiative builds on the NEPAD Peer Review Mechanism. On the OECD side, it extends the OECD's existing Peer Review Mechanism for assessing donor performance, which in recent years has taken some steps to consider the issue of policy coherence.

Ultimately, however, the real obstacles to more coherent policy towards Africa on the part of the G8 and other developed countries are not technical but political. Africa's interests, and the harmful impacts of G8 policy on Africa, need to be pushed higher up the international political agenda.

One way to help achieve this would be through the establishment of a new G8/Africa Forum. This would replace the current unstructured dialogue between G8 and African leaders and become a formal and permanent part of the annual G8 Summit. This Forum should bring together political leaders from the G8 and Africa, as well as the UN Secretary General, and the heads of the IFIs and the African Development Bank. The purpose of the Forum would be to look at the implementation of existing commitments, particularly at 'coherence' issues. The UNECA/OECD-DAC biennial report – a checklist of commitments made to Africa and of progress in implementing them – should be a central focus of discussions at the Forum. To ensure that it is taken seriously at the very highest levels within Africa and the G8, the report should be signed off by the UN Secretary General and presented by him to the G8/Africa Forum. G8 countries should be required to respond in detail to the report at the following G8 summit.

More coherent G8 policy towards Africa could also be facilitated by better structures for making policy within G8 countries. A number of developed country governments have taken steps to improve the overall coherence of their policies towards Africa and other poorer parts of the world. Sweden, for example, has established an integrated global development policy, involving very close coordination between government departments and systematic reporting to the Swedish Parliament (Government of Sweden, 2002). A similar development is underway in the Netherlands. At the same time, Denmark, the Netherlands and Norway have all produced reports on their contribution to MDG8. Amongst G8 countries, the UK Government has set up the innovative Africa Conflict Prevention Pool, to promote more coherent policies towards violent conflict on the continent (DFID/MOD/FCO, 2004). The UK Government has also been praised by the OECD-DAC for its commitment to mainstream development issues and to give them high priority in UK decision-making. The establishment of a separate Department for International Development in 1997, headed by a Cabinet Minister, is seen as a critical structural reform that helped to ensure this (OECD, 2001).

The initiatives taken by Sweden, Denmark, the Netherlands, Norway and the UK are all worth serious study. In various ways, and to varying degrees, these countries have sought to make international development considerations a higher priority within their respective governments. But there is much more that countries could do to reduce any adverse effects of their policies on African and other poor countries. For example, G8 countries could subject certain key policy areas – such as trade, investment or arms exports – to a 'development audit', in the same way that policies are now often assessed and evaluated in terms of their environmental impact. This work might be carried out by existing or specially created parliamentary committees.

G8 countries should:

■ Establish a new G8/Africa Forum – bringing together political leaders from the G8 and Africa, as well as the UN Secretary General, and the heads of the IFIs and the African Development Bank – and make this a permanent part of the G8 Summit.

- Make the UNECA/OECD-DAC biennial report – a checklist of commitments made to Africa and of progress in implementing them – a central focus of discussions at the G8/Africa Forum, and respond in detail to the report.

- Subject important areas of government policy – for example on trade, investment and arms exports – to a comprehensive 'development audit'.

2005 represents a real opportunity to make substantive progress on these 'coherence' issues that matter so much to Africa. The UK Government has the presidencies of the EU and the G8 in this year, and has already indicated that Africa will be a top priority for international action. The Commission for Africa, set up by the UK Government, will report in early 2005. The September UN Review Conference on progress towards the MDGs will also ensure that development issues and the needs of Africa will remain a central focus of international political attention. And 2005 marks the twentieth anniversary of Live Aid, encouraging a much wider group of people to engage with issues around Africa and global justice – perhaps some for the first time – including through the NGO Campaign 'Make Poverty History'.

This report is a contribution to this important and ongoing debate. Its analysis and policy recommendations are designed to help promote better policy towards Africa on the part of G8 countries, and to allow Africans a better chance of securing a more peaceful, prosperous and democratic future for their continent.

References

Introduction

AAPPG (2004) *Averting Catastrophe: AIDS in 21st century Africa*

African Union (2004) *Statement by His Excellency Joaquim Alberto Chissano on African Unity Day* 25 May

Amoako K Y (2003) *Poverty reduction and the MDGs: What does the HIV/AIDS epidemic imply?* Speech to the Joint ADB/ECA Symposium, 2 June 2003, available at http://www.uneca.org/eca_resources/Speeches/amoako/2003/060203speech_amoako.htm

Barnett T and Whiteside A (2002) *AIDS in the Twenty-First Century: Disease and globalisation* Palgrave Macmillan

Bayart J F, Ellis S and Hibou B (1999) *The Criminalization of the State in Africa* James Currey

Bermejo A (2004) 'HIV/AIDS in Africa – International responses to the pandemic' *New Economy* 11(3)

Brown G (2004) 'The challenges of 2005' *New Economy* 11(3)

Chabal P and Daloz J-P (1999) *Africa Works: Disorder as political instrument* James Currey

Cilliers J (2004) *Human security in Africa – a conceptual framework for review* African Human Security Initiative

de Waal A (2004) 'Rethinking aid – developing a human security package for Africa' *New Economy* 11(3)

DFID (2005) *Why we need to work more effectively in fragile states* DFID

Dowden R (2004) 'The state of the African state' *New Economy* 11(3)

Elbe S (2003) *Strategic implications of HIV/AIDS* International Institute for Strategic Studies, Oxford University Press

Ellis S (2004) 'Africa's Wars: The historical context' *New Economy* 11(3)

Gordon D (2001), *Plague upon plague: AIDS and violent conflict in Africa* Remarks at United States Institute for Peace Current Issues Briefing Panel, Washington DC, 8 May, available at http://www.usip.org/events/pre2002/plague_cib.pdf

Herbst J and Mills G (2003) *The future of Africa: A new order in sight?* International Institute for Strategic Studies, quoting from the United Nations Regional Information Network (IRIN), 13 March

HRW (2004) *World Report 2004* Human Rights Watch

Institute for Security Studies (2003) *AIDS, Security and Governance in Southern Africa*

Jackson R (1990) *Quasi-states: Sovereignty, international relations and the Third World* Cambridge University Press

Juma M (2004) 'Africa's governance audit: The African Peer Review Mechanism' *New Economy* 11(3)

Karikari K (2004) 'Press freedom in Africa: Challenges and opportunities' *New Economy* 11(3)

Kpundeh S and Levy B (2004) *Building State Capacity in Africa* World Bank

New Economy (2004) 'A new deal for Africa' *New Economy* 11(3)

New Partnership for Africa's Development (2001) Available at http://www.uneca.org/nepad/nepad.pdf

Prime Minister's Strategy Unit (2005) Countries at risk of instability project, available at http://www.strategy.gov.uk/output/Page5426.asp

Rotberg R (2002) 'The new nature of nation-state failure' *The Washington Quarterly* 25(3):85-96

Rotberg R (2003) *State failure and state weakness in a time of terror* World Peace Foundation

Straw J (2002) *Failed and failing states* Speech given at the European Research Institute, University of Birmingham, 6 September, available at http://www.eri.bham.ac.uk/jstraw.htm

The Nation (2000) 'AIDS accounts for 75 per cent of police officers deaths' *The Nation* 27 November

UNAIDS (2004) *AIDS epidemic update*, December 2004, available at http://www.unaids.org/wad2004/report.html

UNDP (2003) *Human Development Report* Oxford University Press

UNICEF (2005) *Childhood Under Threat: The state of the world's children 2005*, available at http://www.unicef.org/sowc05/english/index.html

United Nations Economic Commission for Africa (2004) *Striving for good governance in Africa* UNECA

US National Intelligence Council (2002) *The Next Wave of HIV/AIDS: Nigeria, Ethiopia, Russia, India, and China* Available at http://www.fas.org/irp/nic/hiv-aids.html

Van de Walle N (2001) *African economies and the politics of permanent crisis, 1979-1999* Cambridge University Press

World Bank, *Low Income Countries under Stress (Licus) initiative* Available at http://www1.worldbank.org/operations/licus/

Chapter 1

ActionAid (2003) *Towards effective partnership: Untie aid* ActionAid Alliance

ActionAid (2004) *Money talks – how aid conditions continue to drive utility privatisation in poor countries* ActionAid Alliance

Amoako K Y (2004) 'The capable state' *New Economy* 11(3)

Bermejo A (2004) 'HIV/AIDS in Africa – international responses to the pandemic' *New Economy* 11(3)

Brown G (2004) 'The challenges of 2005 – forging a new compact for Africa' *New Economy* 11(3)

CIDSE and Caritas Internationalis (2004) *PRSP as theatre – backstage policy-making and the future of the PRSP approach*

DAC (2004) *Implementing the 2001 DAC Recommendation on untying official development assistance to the least developed countries*

De Waal A (2004) 'Rethinking aid – developing a human security package for Africa' *New Economy* 11(3)

DFID (2000) *Eliminating world poverty: Making globalisation work for the poor* White Paper on International Development, December

DFID (2004) *Poverty Reduction Budget Support* A DFID policy paper, DFID

DFID (2005) *Why we need to work more effectively in fragile states* DFID

DFID/HM Treasury/FCO (2004) *Partnerships for poverty reduction: Changing aid conditionality* DFID

Dollar D (2001) *Aid and reform in Africa* July http://www.worldbank.org/research/aid/africa.release/aid.htm

HM Treasury (2004) *International Finance Facility proposal* HM Treasury

IDA/IMF (2004) *HIPC status of implementation report* IDA/IMF

Jubilee (2004) *Jubilee Research* Available at http://www.jubileeresearch.org/hipc/progress_report/countrynominal.htm

Kapoor S (2004) *The IMF, gold sales and multilateral debt cancellation* Jubilee Research for Debt and Development Coalition Ireland

Killick T (1998) *Aid and the political economy of policy change* Routledge and Overseas Development Institute

Killick T (2002) *The streamlining of IMF conditionality: Aspirations, reality and repercussions* A report for the Department for International Development

Mepham D and Cooper J (2004) *Human rights and global responsibility: an international agenda for the UK* ippr

OECD/DAC (2001) Recommendations available at www.oecd.org/dataoecd/14/56/1885476.pdf

Oxfam (2004) *Paying the price – why rich countries must invest now in a war on poverty* Oxfam Briefing Paper Oxfam

Rome Declaration (2003) Available at http://siteresources.worldbank.org/NEWS/ Resources/HarmRomeDeclaration2_25pdf

Sachs *et al.* (2004) *Ending Africa's poverty trap* UN Millennium Project

Van de Walle (2001) *African economies and the politics of permanent crisis, 1979– 1999* Cambridge University Press

War on Want/PCS (2004) *Profiting from poverty – privatisation consultants, DFID and public services* War on Want, Public and Commercial Services Union

Chapter 2

ActionAid (2004) *Trade Traps: Why EU/ACP Economic Partnership Agreements pose a threat to Africa's development*

Benn H (2004) *Living up to our Promises: Helping developing countries to capture the gains from trade* Speech by the UK Secretary of State for International Development to the Royal Institute for International Affairs, 21 July, 2004

Bermejo A (2004) 'HIV/AIDS in Africa – International responses to the pandemic' *New Economy* 11(3)

Brenton P and Ikezuki T (2004) *The initial and potential impact of preferential access to the US Market under the African Growth and Opportunity Act* World Bank Working Paper 3262, World Bank

CIPR (2002) *Integrating intellectual property rights and development policy* Report of the Commission on Intellectual Property Rights and Development, CIPR

Corrales-Leal W, Sugathan M and Primack D (2003) *Spaces for development policy: Revisiting special and differential treatment* International Centre for Trade and Sustainable Development

DTI (2004) *Making globalisation a force for good* Department for Trade and Industry White Paper, DTI

Gillson I (2004) *Developed country cotton subsidies and developing countries: unravelling the impacts on Africa*

Goodison P and Stoneman C (2004) *Trade, development and cooperation: is the EU helping Africa?* Paper for ICS/JCAS/JSAS/ROAPE Conference 10-12 September

Green D (2004) 'Commodities and the WTO' *Bridges*, November

IMF (2003) *Financing of losses from preference erosion: Note on issues raised by developing countries in the Doha Round*, Communication to the WTO from the International Monetary Fund WT/TF/COH/14, 14 February

Kinnock G (2003) *Reshaping European partnerships – what future for the ACP?* Speech to the Overseas Development Institute, 17 September

Minot N and Daniels L (2002) *Impact of global cotton markets on rural poverty in Benin* International Food Policy Research Institute

ODI (2004) *Understanding the impact of cotton subsidies on developing countries* Available at http://www.odi.org.uk/publications/cotton_report/cotton_report.pdf

Oxfam (2002a) *Rigged rules and double standards – trade, globalisation and the fight against poverty* Oxfam International

Oxfam (2002b) *The great EU sugar scam: How Europe's sugar regime is devastating livelihoods in the developing world* Oxfam briefing paper 27, available at http://www.oxfam.org.uk/what_we_do/issues/trade/downloads/bp27_sugar.pdf

Oxfam (2004a) *Finding the moral fibre: Why reform is urgently needed for a fair cotton trade* Oxfam briefing paper, available at http://www.oxfam.org.uk/what_we_do/issues/trade/downloads/bp69_cotton.pdf

Oxfam (2004b) *Dumping on the world: How EU sugar policies hurt poor countries* Oxfam briefing paper, available at http://www.oxfam.org/eng/pdfs/bp61_sugar_dumping.pdf

Page S (2004) *Assessing the poverty impact of the Doha Development Agenda: Preference erosion: helping countries to adjust* Overseas Development Institute

Rodrik D (2001) *The global governance of trade as if development really mattered* Background paper, United Nations Development Programme

Stevens C (2003) 'Food trade and food policy in Sub-Saharan Africa: Old myths and new challenges' *Development Policy Review* 21(5)

Stevens C and Kennan J (2004) *Making trade preferences more effective* Institute of Development Studies, available at http://www.ids.ac.uk/ids/global/pdfs/CSJKTradePreferences.pdf

Thurston J (2002) *How to reform the CAP: A guide to the politics of European agriculture* Foreign Policy Centre

Tibaijuka A (2004) 'Food security in Africa' in *New Economy* 11(3): A New Deal for Africa

World Bank (2000) *World Development Indicators* World Bank

World Bank (2003) *Breaking the conflict trap: civil war and development policy* World Bank

Chapter 3

Amnesty International (2002) *Russian weapons fuel African conflicts* Available at http://web.amnesty.org/web/web.nsf/pages/ttt3_russian

Amnesty International (2003) *A catalogue of failures: G8 arm exports and human rights violations* Available at http://amnesty-news.c.tclk.net/maaa5LpaaX4VgbdLrlzb/

DFID (2001) *The causes of conflict in Africa* Department for International Development

Foreign and Commonwealth Office (2002) *Strategic export controls report 2002* Available at http://www.fco.gov.uk/servlet/Front?pagename=OpenMarket/ Xcelerate/ShowPage&c=Page&cid=1056723941828

GIIS (2003) *Small arms survey 2003 – Development denied* Graduate Institute of International Studies, Oxford University Press

GIIS (2004) *Small arms survey 2004 – Rights at risk* Graduate Institute of International Studies, Oxford University Press

Global Witness (2003) *The usual suspects: Liberia's weapons and mercenaries in Cote D'Ivoire and Sierra Leone* Available at http://www.globalwitness.org/reports/ show.php/en.00026.htlm

Grimmett R F (2004) *Conventional arms transfers to developing nations, 1996-2003* Congressional Research Service report to US Congress

Human Rights Watch (2005) *World Report 2005*

IISS (2004) *Armed Conflict Database* International Institute of Strategic Studies, available at http://acd.iiss.org/armedconflict/MainPages/dsp_ ConflictSummary.asp?ConflictID-157

Klare M (2004) 'The deadly connection – paramilitary bands, small arms diffusion and state failure' in Rotburg R (ed) *When states fail: causes and consequences* Princeton University Press

Mkutu K (2003) *Pastoral conflict and small arms: The Kenya-Uganda border* Saferworld

Nathan L (2004) *The Four Horseman of the Apocalypse: The structural causes of crisis and violence in Africa* Development Research Centre LSE

Palan R (2003) *The offshore world: Sovereign markets, virtual places and nomad millionaires* Cornell University Press

RAID (2004) *Unanswered questions: companies, conflict and the Democratic Republic of Congo* Available at http://www.oecdwatch.org/docs/RAID%20full%20DRC% 20report.pdf

Stewart F (2001) 'Horizontal inequalities: A neglected dimension of development' *Working Paper 1* Centre for Research on Inequality, Human Security and Ethnicity, Queen Elizabeth House

UN (1998) *The causes of conflict and the promotion of durable peace and sustainable development in Africa* Report of the Secretary General, United Nations

UN Panel (2002a) *Final report of the UN Panel of Experts on the illegal exploitation of national resources and other forms of wealth of the Democratic Republic of Congo* S/2002/1146, 16 October 2002

UN Panel (2002b) *Report of the Panel of Experts on Liberia in accordance with paragraph 16 of resolution 1458 (2003) S2003/498*, 24 April, available at www. un.orgDocs/sc/committees/LiberiaSeleng.htm

World Bank (2003) *Breaking the conflict trap: civil war and development policy* World Bank

Chapter 4

Amnesty International and Global Witness (2004) *Déjà vu: diamond industry still failing to deliver on promises* Available at http://web.amnesty.org/library/pdf/POL340082004ENGLISH/$File/POL3400804.pdf

Amoako KY (2004) 'The Capable State', *New Economy* 11(3)

Ballentine K and Sherman J (eds) (2003) *The political economy of armed conflict: Beyond greed and grievance* International Peace Academy: Lynne Rienner Publishers

Banfield J, Haufler V and Lilly D (2003) *Transnational corporations in conflict prone zones: Public policy responses and a framework for action* International Alert

Bannon I and Collier P (2003) 'Natural resources and conflict: What can we do?' in Bannon I and Collier P (eds) *Natural Resources and Violent Conflict*, World Bank Report, World Bank

BBC (19 February 2003) *Chiluba loses immunity appeal* Available at http://news.bbc.co.uk/1/hi/world/africa/2779615.stm

Bray J (2003) *Facing up to corruption 2003* Control Risks Group

Control Risks Group (2002) *Facing up to corruption: Survey results 2002* Available at http://www.crg.com/images/pdf/Control_Risks_Global_Corruption_Survey_2002_Results.pdf

Corner House (2000) *Corruption, privatisation and multinationals* Briefing Paper 19

Corner House (2003) *Underwriting bribery: Export credit agencies and corruption* Briefing Paper 30

Eigen P (2002) *Controlling Corruption: A key to development-oriented trade* Carnegie Endowment for International Peace

European Commission (2003) *Forest Law Enforcement, Governance and Trade (FLEGT): Proposal for an EU action plan* Available at http://europa.eu.int/comm/development/body/theme/forest/initiative/docs/Doc1-FLEGT_en.pdf#zoom=100

Extractive Industries Transparency Initiative, available at http://www.eitransparency.org/

FERN, Greenpeace and WWF (2004) *Facing Reality: How to halt the import of illegal timber in the EU*

Ganesan A and Vines A (2004) 'Engine of War: Resources, Greed and the Predatory State' in HRW *World Report 2004* Human Rights Watch

Global Witness (2002) *Logging off: How the Liberian timber industry fuels Liberia's humanitarian disaster and threatens Sierra Leone* Global Witness

Global Witness (2004) *Broken Vows: Exposing the 'Loupe' holes in the diamond industry's efforts to prevent the trade in conflict diamonds* Global Witness, available at http://www.globalwitness.org/reports/show/php/en.00050.html

Goredema C and Botha A (2004) *African commitments to combating organised crime and terrorism* African Human Security Initiative

Gray C W and Kaufmann D (1998) *Corruption and development* World Bank working paper: Finance and Development, World Bank

Gupta S, Davoodi H and Alonso-Terme R (1998) *Does corruption affect income inequality and poverty?* IMF Working Paper, IMF

IMF (2001) *US Anti-money laundering practices* Available at http://www.imf.org/external/np/mae/aml/2001/eng/110801.htm

Levi M (2002) *Controlling the International Money Trail: A multi-level cross-national public policy review* Available at http://www.regard.ac.uk/research_findings/L216252037/report.pdf

Mepham D and Cooper J (2004) *Human rights and global responsibility: An international agenda for the UK* ippr

NEPAD (2001) *The new partnership for Africa's development* Para 1, NEPAD

OECD (1997) *Convention on combating bribery of foreign public officials in international business transactions* Available at http://www.oecd.org/document/21/0,2340,en_2649_34859_2017813_1_1_1_1,00.html

OECD (2003) *Business approaches to combating corrupt practices* Available at http://www.oecd.org/dataoecd/63/57/2638716.pdf

OECD (2004) *Steps taken and planned future actions by participating countries to ratify and the implement the convention on combating bribery of foreign public officials in international business transactions* Available at http://www.oecd.org/dataoecd/50/33/1827022.pdf

Royal Institute for International Affairs (2003) *Forest governance and trade: Illegal logging stakeholder update meeting* Summary of a meeting held on 2 December 2003

Transparency International (2002) *Bribe Payers Index 2002* Available at www.transparency.org/cpi/2002/bpi2002.en.html

Transparency International (2004) *Global corruption report 2004* Available at www.globalcorruptionreport.org

United Nations Office of Drugs and Crime, see http://www.unodc.org/unodc/en/crime_signatures_corruption.html

UN Panel (2002) *Final report of the UN Panel of Experts on the illegal exploitation of national resources and other forms of wealth of the Democratic Republic of Congo* S/2002/1146, 16 October

UN Security Council (2000) *Report of the Panel of Experts pursuant to UN Security Council Resolution 1306 in relation to Sierra Leone*

World Bank Operations Evaluation Department (2003) *Evaluation of the World Bank Group's activities in the extractives industries* 21 January

World Bank (2003) *Breaking the conflict trap: civil war and development policy* World Bank

Zhang H (2000) 'Corruption, Economic Growth and Macroeconomic Volatility' *Perspectives* 2(1)

Chapter 5

Blair T (2004) PM speech on climate change, 14 September, available at www. number-10.gov.uk/output/Page6333.asp

Burton I *et al.* (1999) *Come hell or high water – integrating climate change vulnerability and adaptation into Bank work* World Bank

Burton I *et al.* (2002) *From impacts assessment to adaptation priorities: the shaping of adaptation policy* Climate Policy 2

Burton I *et al.* (2004) *Look before you leap: a risk management approach for incorporating climate change adaptation into World Bank operations* World Bank

Dunn S (2000) *Micropower: The next electrical era* Paper 151, Worldwatch

DFID (2004a) 'Key sheet 10: Climate change in Africa' in *Climate Change and Poverty* DFID

DFID (2004b) *African climate report: A report commissioned by the UK Government to review African climate science, policy and options for action* DFID

Economist (2004) 'Kyoto a-go-go', *The Economist Global Agenda* 30 September

European Environment Agency (2004) *Greenhouse gas emission trends and projections in Europe 2004* EEA Report No 5/2004, EEA

G8 Renewables Task Force (2001) Available at http://www.worldenergy.org/wec-geis/focus/renew/g8.asp

Hall K (2004) *Japan says won't meet Kyoto targets reducing greenhouse gases without policy changes* Associated Press, 15 May

Hampton K (2005) *Catalysing commitment: A paper for the International Taskforce on Climate Change* ippr

House of Lords (2004) *The EU and Climate Change* 30th Report of Session 2003-04, EU Committee, 10 November

Huq S *et al.* (2003) *Mainstreaming adaptation to climate change in least developed countries* International Institute for Environment and Development

Huq S (2005) *Adaptation: A paper for the International Taskforce on Climate Change* ippr

IPCC (2001a) *Climate Change 2001: The scientific basis* Intergovernmental Panel on Climate Change

IPCC (2001b) *Africa* Intergovernmental Panel on Climate Change

IPS (2004) *Poor and vulnerable countries demand compensation* Inter Press Service News Agency, 6 December http://ipsnews.net/africa/interna.asp?idnews=26561

Juniper T (2003) 'Strengthening the link between climate change, international development and social justice' in Foley (ed) *Sustainability and Social Justice* ippr

MATCH http://match-info.net/

Meyer A (2000) *Contraction and Convergence: The global solution to climate change*, Green Books Schumacher Briefing

Mitchell C and Woodman B (2004) *The Burning Question: is the UK on course for a low carbon economy?* ippr

nef (2003) *Free riding on the climate: The possibility of legal, economic and trade restrictive measures to tackle inaction on global warming* New Economics Foundation

nef (2004) *Cast adrift: How the rich are leaving the poor to sink in a warming world* New Economics Foundation

Radford T (2004) 'Climate change claims flawed, says study' *The Guardian*, 9 November

Retallack S (2005) *Setting a long-term climate objective: A paper for the International Taskforce on Climate Change* ippr

Simms A (2001) *An environmental war economy: The lessons of ecological debt and global warming* New Economics Foundation

Simms A *et al.* (2004) *Up in Smoke? Threats from, and responses to, the impact of global warming on human development* New Economics Foundations/Working Group on Climate Change and Development

World Bank (2004) *Striking a Better Balance: The Extractive Industries Review*

Conclusion

Amoako KY (2004) 'The capable state' *New Economy* 11(3)

CGD (2004) *Ranking the rich: The 2004 commitment to development index* Available at http://www.cgdev.org/rankingtherich/home.html

DFID/MOD/FCO (2004) *The Africa conflict prevention Pool: An information document* Available at http://www.dfid.gov.uk/pubs/files/acppinfodoc.pdf

Government of Sweden (2002) *An integrated Swedish globalisation policy for equitable economic development* Government of Sweden

IDC (2004) *The Commission for Africa and policy coherence for development: First do no harm* House of Commons International Development Committee

OECD (2001) *United Kingdom: Development Co-operation Review* Available at http://www.oecd.org/dataoecd/38/14/30716216.pdf

Picciotto R (2004) *Policy coherence for development* Memorandum submitted to the International Development Select Committee, October 2004